Trust
Builders

Trust
Builders

How You Can Restore
the Foundation of
a Lasting Marriage

RON R. LEE, *General Editor*
and GARY J. OLIVER, PH.D.

SERVANT PUBLICATIONS
ANN ARBOR, MICHIGAN

Vine Books is an imprint of Servant Publications especially designed to serve
evangelical Christians.

All Scripture quotations, unless indicated, are taken from the HOLY BIBLE, NEW
INTERNATIONAL VERSION®. © 1973, 1978, 1984 by International Bible
Society. Used by permission of Zondervan Publishing House. All rights reserved.

Dr. Oliver's commentaries are published in association with the literary agency of
Alive Communications, Inc., 1465 Kelly Johnson Blvd., Suite 320, Colorado
Springs, CO 80920.

The couples portrayed in these true stories have generously given their full permission for these stories to be published.

Published by Servant Publications
P.O. Box 8617
Ann Arbor, Michigan 48107

Cover design: Paul Higdon
Cover photograph: © Paul Barton / The Stock Market. Used by permission.

99 00 01 02 10 9 8 7 6 5 4 3 2 1

Printed in the United States of America
ISBN 1-56955-178-2

Library of Congress Cataloging-in-Publication Data

Trust builders : how you can restore the foundation of a lasting marriage / Ron R.
Lee, general editor and Gary J. Oliver.
    p.   cm.
ISBN 1-56955-178-2 (alk. paper)
1. Marriage—United States—Psychological aspects. 2. Trust. 3. Reconcilliation.
4. Marriage—Religious aspects—Christianity. 5. Reconcilliation—Religious aspects—Christianity. 6. Married people—Religious life. I. Lee, Ron R. II. Oliver,
Gary J.
HQ734.T87   1999   99-42804
306.81—dc21   CIP

Contents

Acknowledgments

No one looks forward to reliving painful experiences. Yet, the thirteen couples in this book have revisited the darkest days of their marriages to show there is hope even in the center of life's tragedies. I am indebted to these couples, whose stories prove that God is still in control. I'd also like to thank the writers who translated the oral narratives into written form.

I have the highest regard for Gary J. Oliver, Ph.D., whose insightful and compassionate counsel points the way to healing. He brings to bear the wisdom of Scripture and the best of the helping professions.

Finally, my sincere thanks go to the editorial staff, both past and present, of *Marriage Partnership* magazine. My hat is off to Barbara Calvert, Louise Ferrebee, Annette LaPlaca, Marian Liautaud, Lori McCullough, Elizabeth Cody Newenhuyse, Melissa Parks, and Caryn Rivadeneira. The stories in this book first appeared in *Marriage Partnership,* and they would not have made it onto the printed page without the efforts of these dedicated professionals.

—Ron R. Lee
General Editor

Acknowledgments

I would like to thank the couples who had the courage and generosity to allow their stories to be told. While they were going through pain and despair, they had little idea how God would use their experience to strengthen their own marriages, let alone those of the thousands of other couples who would have the opportunity to walk through their experiences with them through the pages of *Marriage Partnership* magazine and this book.

After first reading through each one of the stories and praying about what kinds of observations might be most helpful to the readers, I realized that, given the wide range of problems and issues presented, it would be useful to have other clinical eyes look at some of them. My sincere appreciation goes to those who gave me their perspective on some of the stories: Dr. Steve Lee, chairman of the Department of Psychology at Huntington College, Huntington, Indiana; Alan Tyson, chaplain at St. Mary's Hospital, Rogers, Arkansas; and Dr. David Brisben, Dr. John Carmack, Carrie Oliver, and Nancy Schmer, my colleagues at The Center for Marriage and Family Studies and in the graduate program in Marriage and Family Therapy at John Brown University. A final expression of appreciation goes to the donors who have made The Center for Marriage and Family Studies a reality, and to my administrative assistant, Jan Phillips, for helping to coordinate this project and for her great sense of humor.

—Gary J. Oliver, Ph. D.

Introduction
Ron R. Lee, General Editor

Think how troubling life would be without a basic level of trust. Is the utility company charging me for more electricity than I'm actually using? Is the supermarket checker scanning some of my items twice? Is my business partner utilizing the start-up capital according to the terms of our agreement? If we couldn't depend on others, we'd spend the bulk of our time checking up on them. Trust makes daily life much easier to navigate.

Likewise, marriage relies on trust. As wives and husbands, we depend on one another to keep our word, to seek each other's welfare, to live according to the vows we made. Trust, like breathing or riding a bicycle, is something we don't even think about. That is, until it's broken.

Substance abuse, adultery, neglect, pornography addiction, secrecy, broken promises. It's easy to see how human failures undermine marriage. And beyond a spouse's betrayal, we can feel forsaken by God when a daughter is born with a severe disability, when a home is destroyed in a natural disaster, when a series of medical emergencies leads to bankruptcy, when a son dies in his father's arms. God doesn't always protect us from the pain of undeserved suffering. If we can't count on a spouse always to do the right thing, and if even God seems unwilling to spare us the pain of senseless loss, then what good is trust?

Because life's struggles have far-reaching effects on our faith and our marriages, this book shows how trust can be restored. Thirteen couples tell how they overcame circumstances that would push most marriages over the brink. These couples discovered the power of God's grace to restore hope, to bring reconciliation, and to heal their relationships.

Adding to the impact of each couple's story, Gary J. Oliver, Ph.D., executive director of The Center for Marriage and Family Studies and Professor of Psychology and Practical Theology at John Brown University, recommends additional steps to take in the midst of marital crises. With God as the third partner in your marriage there is reason to trust again.

Introduction
Gary J. Oliver, Ph.D.

Where did you learn how to handle the inevitable set-backs, crises, and losses of life? Who taught you? If you're at all like most of us, you didn't learn how. No one taught you. You probably learned to do what most of us do: run, hide, try to avoid problems. Or if you find yourself stuck in the middle of one you can't avoid, get through it as soon as possible and don't look back.

Difficult and draining times can produce significant stress on a marriage. When times are tough it becomes easier to be negative and critical. When things go wrong it becomes much easier to justify and rationalize your own behavior and to blame the problems on someone else. Often that "someone else" is your spouse. Stress and pressure bring existing weaknesses to the surface and can make them appear larger than life.

Tough times also provide couples with an opportunity to pull together, to join hands, to share hearts, to pray and praise together, and in the process to experience a greater depth of love and trust than you might ever have imagined.

This is a book about real couples who have come face to face with some of the most difficult, challenging issues that any marriage could face and who have responded as most normal people would. Yet in every case—despite mistakes, setbacks, sins, failure, and overwhelming losses—they didn't quit. They emerged, in some cases scarred, but always as conquerors.

God is faithful. When circumstances tempt you to wallow in despair, reread even a couple of these stories and you will hear that there is help, there is hope—a hope that was paid for at the cross, guaranteed by an empty tomb, recorded in God's infallible Word, and testified to by the men and women whose stories you are about to read.

The Bible makes it clear that, while God loves us just the way we are, he loves us too much to leave us that way. Because he loves us he wants to see us become "conformed to the likeness of his son" (Rom 8:29). Because he loves us he wants to help us "in all things grow up into him who is the Head, that is, Christ ..." (Eph 4:15).

This growing-up process involves change, which sometimes comes through crises, problems, setbacks, sin, mistakes, and failures. Change can be simple, but it is seldom easy and rarely painless. Change takes time, energy, the willingness to admit our need, the courage to face our failures and fears, and the faith to believe that in the midst of uncertainty our God will be faithful. In over thirty years of being a counselor I've never heard anyone say, "I want to stagnate, remain immature, play it safe, stay stuck." Yet that is exactly what we are choosing to do when we avoid change and fight hard to stay the same.

For many people change is something negative. It suggests inferiority, inadequacy, and failure. No wonder so many of us run from or resist the idea of change.

I've met a few people who have bought into the myth that born-again evangelical Christians are always stable and strong, have all the right answers, and don't make mistakes. But let's face it: When you boil the Christian life down to the basics, the name of the game is change. People who want to learn, who are willing to look at themselves in the mirror before grabbing the binoculars to look at others, who refuse to stay in a rut, and who make time to listen for the still, small voice of the Holy Spirit are the people whom God is free to use, to bless, to honor. They are the ones who know what it means to be "more than conquerors" (Rom 8:37).

In many ways what you hold in your hand is a handbook of solutions. The reality of these stories flies in the face of platitudes and mundane spiritual banalities.

As you read each one of these fascinating stories you may be tempted to tell yourself, "This will never happen to me," or "These were just super-strong people." But they were (and are) just ordinary people. Ordinary men and women who decided to believe, who decided to trust, who decided to get up one more time than they were knocked down, who decided that, against all odds, truth just might make a difference. God's promises just might be true.

Chapter 1

Alcoholism
by Beth Spring

Dave: I met Elsie at a Fourth of July party. She arrived late, and she certainly made it more interesting. We were engaged by Thanksgiving.

Elsie: Shortly after we met, we went back to school. Dave was at Yale, and I was studying nursing in Pittsburgh, so we didn't see each other very often. When I visited him, I noticed that he was drinking a lot. But I thought, "Well, he's just a college guy. When we get married he'll shape up." I had no idea what a drinking problem looked like.

Dave: I wanted Elsie to be impressed with me, so I tried not to drink excessively when she visited me at Yale. I didn't want her to see any weaknesses in me. One thing alcoholics have in common is low self-esteem. To cover up my own feelings of inadequacy, I joined a lot of organizations. Usually I was in the position that controlled the liquor cabinet.

Elsie: We got married in 1966 and were living in Michigan City, Indiana. Almost right away I realized how serious Dave's drinking problem was. The second or third night we were there, Dave said he was going to his company basketball game and out with the guys afterward for a few beers. He told me, "I'll be home around nine o'clock." I stayed in the apartment.

Dave didn't come home at nine or ten or eleven or twelve. By midnight, I was beside myself. He finally came in at one.

I was angry and frightened. But the next day I consoled myself by thinking, "He's not going to do that again." And then it would happen again. I fooled myself over and over. I didn't know who to talk to or where to go. I didn't want anyone to know, so I kept it secret.

Dave: The alcoholic has good intentions. I really intended to have just one or two beers and then go home. But after one or two drinks, an alcoholic feels as if he is glued to the barstool. Next thing you know, it's midnight or 1 A.M. and the bar is closing.

I could tell I was hurting our relationship, but I didn't know what to do about it. I couldn't break the cycle of drinking beer after beer, as many as twenty-four beers in a single evening, so I began to justify it. Drinking was more important to me than anything else. The one bright spot in our marriage was the birth of our son Hector in 1967.

Elsie: When Hector was born, Dave came into the hospital room and sat down next to my bed. He said, "I'm going to give up drinking, because I'm so thrilled." It felt so good to hear him say that.

Dave: I stayed away from alcohol for about six months. But I was doing it for the wrong reasons: For my wife and my new baby, not for myself. During that time I became progressively harder to live with and more grouchy.

I really wanted a good family life, and I couldn't understand why it wasn't happening. I knew nothing about the work involved in making a good marriage. We weren't reading books on the subject, we didn't go to church, we had no channel open to receive that kind of input.

After six months I started drinking again. The excuse came when we moved into a farmhouse in Baroda, Michigan. To reward the friends who helped us move, I bought some beer. And it wouldn't have been polite to let them drink alone, would it?

Elsie: It struck fear into my heart to hear Dave say, "I'm going to have just a couple of beers." After that, all the old patterns of behavior returned.

The late nights really bothered me. Occasionally he would stay out until four or five in the morning or not come home at all for a day or two. It became more and more frequent. Dave also developed physical symptoms—he had a bleeding ulcer. One time he got a gun and said he was going to shoot himself.

We wanted to have another child, and Davie was born in 1970. That is when our marriage really began to deteriorate. I had spent most of my four years of married life staying up all night worrying about Dave. During the day I was exhausted and tried to sleep. We began seeing a psychiatrist, but he understood nothing about alcoholism.

One day Dave said he was going away for the weekend. Davie was a couple of months old, and Hector was two. Right after Dave left, I called my parents and said, "Mom and Dad, come up here and get me. I can't take any more of this and I don't think I can make an eight-hour drive with the boys." They came right away.

Dave: It's hard to name a particular moment when I became an alcoholic. It happened gradually, and it got worse as I tried to reconcile the decent person I thought I was with the indecent actions I had to acknowledge I was doing. I couldn't bring those two together. Finally, a sense of total despair set in.

After Elsie left, I quit my job and just stayed in the house. I felt terrible, so I began saving up pills prescribed by my psychiatrist. I wanted to kill myself, so I swallowed all of them one afternoon and passed out on the kitchen floor. Providentially, the kid from the neighbor's farm happened to walk by the house. He called the rescue squad and they took me to the hospital and pumped out my stomach. Three days later, I woke up. My parents came and took me home.

Both Dave and Elsie were back in Sewickley, Pennsylvania, a suburb of Pittsburgh, where Elsie grew up and where she and Dave had been married. Their separation seemed to be a point of no return, so Elsie filed for divorce. They saw each other only when she dropped off or picked up Hector and Davie after a visit with their dad.

Dave: One time when Elsie came to pick up the boys, Hector tried to push me into her car. He said nothing, but his actions said, "I don't understand this, Dad, and I want you to come home." I went into the house after Elsie left and bawled. This little guy who had no say in it whatsoever was hurting so badly. It hit me like a gunshot.

About one month after I came home, a fellow named John gave me literature about Alcoholics Anonymous (AA) and took me to a meeting. I was willing to try anything.

At the first meeting, I was amazed. Here was a room full of people who, after I got to know them, said, "I've got the same problem you do, and I've got a solution that works." All of a sudden, the dark tunnel I was in seemed to open up. There was hope.

I stopped drinking completely when I began going to AA, and this time I did it for the right reasons. Elsie was gone, so I was doing it for myself and not for her.

Elsie: I had moved out of Mom and Dad's house and was living in an apartment with the boys. The month the divorce was finalized, an old high school friend named Chip came to see me. He popped in one day and said, "Hi. I've become a Christian."

He dragged me to St. Stephen's Episcopal Church to meet the rector, John Guest, and his wife, Kathy. I could see real joy in their lives and an inner confidence about where they were going.

I started going to church on Sunday. Finally I asked Christ into my life. I started telling people about it. At that point, I wasn't thinking about Dave very often.

Dave: I began attending St. Stephen's too, but I went to an early-morning service. I wanted to make sense out of life. I wanted to see a dimension beyond dog-eat-dog and whoever dies with the most toys wins. What I was hearing from John Guest fit in with what I was hearing at AA. The first three steps toward recovery in AA say this: "We are powerless over alcohol. We've come to believe there is a power greater than ourselves. We have made a decision to turn our will and our lives over to the care of God as we understand him." All twelve of AA's steps are consistent with Christian belief.

One night I was watching television in a motel room in Orlando, Florida, where I was working as a management consultant. A Billy Graham crusade came on the screen. I don't remember anything he said, but I remember the closing hymn: "Just as I am, without one plea, O Lamb of God, I come to thee." All of a sudden I realized I didn't have to wait until I was good enough or until I'd learned enough. God wanted to deal with me now.

I stood in the middle of my motel room and said, "Well, God, if you're for real and if you really care, and if I'm not just talking to the wind, then I give up. I've tried to live my life and I'm not happy with the results. I still feel unfulfilled—I feel empty inside. If you want my life, you've got it."

I started reading the Bible, and that became one of the vehicles for reestablishing communication with Elsie.

Elsie: I knew Dave was in AA because at one point he called my parents and asked if he could come and see them. They said that would be fine. He got all dressed up and drove to their house. He was there only ten minutes. He came up to the porch, sat down, and asked them to forgive him for what he had done to me. I was sitting there listening. Then he said, "Thank you very much" and left. My parents were very polite. I think it made more of an impression on me than it did on them. I remember thinking, "It took a lot of nerve to do that."

Dave: Asking her parents for forgiveness fulfilled one of the AA steps toward recovery. AA tells you to take a "complete and fearless moral inventory" of all the things in your life that caused guilt and shame. Then you take steps to address the wrongs you've committed. It's not a one-time event, but something you continue to work on.

Elsie: Another change in Dave's behavior: I told him to come at two on a Saturday afternoon for his weekly visit with the boys, and he showed up on time. Well, that just never happens with an alcoholic. They are totally unreliable.

He was friendly and well-groomed and he didn't have a drink in his hand. We started talking, and he actually listened to me. He seemed to really care about the boys. I had to admit to myself that I was sorry to see him leave. That was scary because our marriage had been so horrible. I didn't want to get involved again, but I liked having him around.

I began telling him about St. Stephen's Church and how excited I was about my faith. Then he told me about AA. We started dating each other again, and finally we began asking each other, "Do you think you still love me?" We started talking seriously about the possibility of remarrying. He was more interested in it than I was, but we both had a growing sense that God wanted us to get back together. It was frightening. But both of us had benefited from sound instruction at church and the support of our new Christian friends.

Neither Dave nor Elsie dated anyone else seriously during the two years they were separated and divorced. They decided to remarry during a typical Saturday-afternoon visit. "The boys were play-

ing on the floor," Elsie recalls, "and we sat in the playroom discussing it."

They asked for both their parents' blessing and got it, albeit reluctantly. John Guest then told them, "Keep your hands off each other, get professional counseling from a Christian counselor, and court each other and do it right this time." Three months later they were ready to set a date.

Elsie: It was John's idea for us to be remarried during a Sunday-morning worship service on April 16, 1972. We stood together and said all the vows. Then every other couple at church stood and did the same thing.

We were just floating, and we floated to Jamaica for a five-day honeymoon. Physically, the honeymoon was wonderful. Once we had made the decision not to have sexual relations until after the remarriage, we stuck with it. I believe God blessed our honeymoon because of that. I felt like a bride.

Dave: The first marriage was so typical. We had stars in our eyes, and we walked down the aisle believing everything would be happy forever. Marrying the same person the second time struck raw terror in my heart. All the way down the aisle I asked myself, "What in the world am I doing? How will I face family and friends if we blow it again?" I knew the pitfalls the second time.

Elsie: The second marriage was so different. There were no more nights out, no more unpredictability. Dave was telling me about his feelings and not running out the door when he became angry. We prayed about things we disagreed on or just sat on them a while. Dave told me once that he dreamed I might leave him again. He never would have told me that before.

At the same time, our marriage wasn't perfect. Our biggest source of conflict was Dave's consulting job. He was away all week and home on the weekends. That went on for the first year of our remarriage, and it was hard on our relationship. But the good thing was I could tell him I was upset about it. He didn't just get quiet or go out the door and drink. We could communicate. Finally, Dave said it was getting harder and harder for him to get on the plane and leave every Sunday night. So he left his job and came home.

An affirmation of the MacKenzies' success in reconciling came in 1975, when twin girls were born to them. In addition, Dave went to seminary. He was ordained in 1979 and accepted a position in Virginia where he began counseling couples and working with the local chapter of AA.

Dave: Whether alcohol plays a part or not, all couples have differences to work out. In marriage counseling, I begin by telling partners that they must let the past remain in the past. What has already happened between them needs to be admitted, forgiven, and left behind.

When I counsel engaged couples, I ask them, "What are your goals for your marriage?" Usually, they look at me as if I just walked in from Mars. For most of them, marriage is the goal. They don't think past the wedding date. They say, "We want to have a house in the country and two cars." I tell them that's an economic goal, not a marital goal. Or they say, "We want four kids." Well, that's a family goal.

I try to get them to think in terms of God's goal for marriage, which is "becoming one." That is the highest priority for a marriage.

Commentary

In 2 Corinthians 11:30 the apostle Paul tells us, "If I must boast, I will boast of the things that show my weakness." Can you imagine someone saying that today? Especially a guy? What kinds of things are you most likely to boast about? What kinds of things do you deny or attempt to cover up and hide? If you are like 99 percent of the people I've worked with your answer is your flaws, your failures, and your weaknesses.

Paul had learned that our God uses failure to give us a taste of our weakness, sinfulness, and wretchedness. He had learned that acknowledging our weakness is the first step on the road to healing, recovery, and health.

It's one thing to hear Paul talk about these ideas. He lived two thousand years ago. It's an entirely different thing to see that reality lived out today. But that is exactly what the story of Dave and Elsie is about. They sound like a normal couple. They dated and they fell in love. While they were dating Elsie had some red flags about Dave's drinking but she was young, in love, and, like many love-struck people before her, rationalized her concerns away.

At this point in their relationship there is something that could have made an enormous difference ... good premarital counseling. Good premarital counseling involves at least six sessions with someone who has been trained to help couples prepare and lay a good foundation for their marriage relationship. It's a scary thought that there is more preparation for a driver's license than for a marriage license. It's possible that the existence of the alcohol problem might have emerged during premarital counseling.

It's true: "One thing alcoholics share in common is low self-esteem." People who feel good about themselves, people who have a clear sense of who they are, people who know what it means to be "in Christ" don't have to medicate themselves and try to anesthetize the pain in their lives. Believe it or not, Dave had good intentions. Most alcoholics do. The problem isn't necessarily how sincere or well-meaning an alcoholic is, the problem is that they have an addiction that distorts their perspective, weakens their will, and dramatically affects their behavior. The blunt reality is if you don't take control of the alcohol it will take control of you. Alcoholism affects everyone it touches, it pervades every aspect of family interaction. Spouses, relatives, and friends reel from the impact of it. Children grow up in an atmosphere of misunderstanding and fear. After years of using alcohol Dave was forced to admit that "drinking was more important to me than anything else."

With the birth of Hector, Dave made a good decision,

but he didn't follow it up with a specific plan. I've worked with thousands of alcoholics who, at one point or another in their addictions, had good intentions. However, good intentions rarely accomplish anything. With the birth of Davie things went from bad to worse. Dave and Elsie did make a good move in reaching out to see a psychiatrist, but unfortunately this highly trained professional didn't understand alcoholism.

If you've never lived with or been around an alcoholic you might not understand what Elsie went through. Life with an active alcoholic is characterized by chaos. Roles become reversed, rules become distorted, promises are broken, and commitments made in the depth of sincerity are betrayed. After awhile it can make you doubt your sanity.

The road Dave walked down was predictable. You can only numb yourself so much. As the alcoholism continued its destructive path, Dave became depressed and suicidal. The negative effect on the kids became more evident as Hector started having problems. Children of alcoholics often feel unloved, insecure, guilty, ashamed, invisible, responsible for the parent's alcoholism, afraid of abuse or violence, embarrassed, isolated, betrayed, and fearful that the alcoholic will become ill or die. They may retreat into roles that help them survive but keep them from growing. Feeling helpless and hopeless, Elsie eventually filed for divorce. It was then that the reality of the problem finally began to set in for Dave.

At this point in his life Dave made another decision

that he followed up with action. He had made many decisions in the past but had failed to make a plan and find the support to help him follow through. This time his decision was different. He chose to attend an Alcoholics Anonymous meeting. "I stopped drinking completely when I began going to AA, and this time I did it for the right reasons." This wasn't just another short-term quick fix. At some level Dave knew that this was about life and death. As he reached out, Dave discovered that help was available to understand and deal with his emotions, especially the emotion of anger. He learned not only how to identify his emotions but also how to communicate them.

When Elsie made the decision to give her heart to Christ and to move from a head knowledge to a heart knowledge of the Savior, God was free to work at a whole new level in her life. Over time Dave made another critical decision—to accept Christ as his personal Lord and Savior. Once again, he followed up this decision with action. He started spending time studying the Bible, he continued working the Twelve Steps of the AA program, one of which involves taking a moral inventory of wrongs you've committed. He then took specific steps to address the wrong: He asked Elsie's parents for forgiveness, not for show, not as window dressing, not as another of the relational cons that many alcoholics are so good at. His outward behavior was a manifestation of the inward changes that were taking place. Dave added discipline to his good intentions. Over time Elsie began to notice the changes.

Dave and Elsie are living proof that God loves to build on our weaknesses, our mistakes, our failures. He takes the ruins of our brave (and at times vain) attempts and fashions the seemingly useless pieces of rubble into a life that brings him praise and honor. Those aren't the building materials that we would use. But our weak wills, inadequate resources, inconsistent efforts, and imperfect vision are being transformed by his power into the finest of building materials out of which he is making something beautiful.

Resources

Stephanie Brown, ed., *Treating Alcoholism* (San Francisco: Jossey-Bass, 1995).

Robert Hemfelt, Frank Minirth, and Paul Meier, *Love Is a Choice: Recovery for Codependent Relationships* (Nashville, Tenn.: Thomas Nelson, 1989).

Bill and Lyndi McCartney, *Sold Out to Each Other* (Nashville, Tenn.: Word, 1999).

Gerald May, *Addiction and Grace* (San Francisco: Harper & Row, 1988).

Les and Leslie Parrott, *Saving Your Marriage Before It Starts* (Grand Rapids, Mich.: Zondervan, 1995).

H. Norman Wright, *Before You Say I Do* (Eugene, Ore.: Harvest House, 1997).

——— *So You're Getting Married* (Ventura, Calif.: Regal, 1985).

Chapter 2

Bankruptcy
by Renae Bottom

M elinda and Tim Inman had known this day would be
difficult, but they hadn't expected such a large crowd
in the courtroom. More than fifty other people were waiting
for the judge to call their names.

There was no exchange of polite conversation. Just being in
bankruptcy court belied a secret so personal that few seemed
comfortable with small talk. When the Inmans' turn came, Tim
walked to the front, then turned and faced the onlookers. He
answered the judge's questions: "Are you Timothy Inman? Is
this your correct address? Are these the debts in question?"

Then the judge addressed the crowd: "Are there creditors
present who wish to present a claim against these debts?" No
one answered. When the judge was satisfied, Tim stepped
down. He and Melinda hurried from the room, glad to escape
the awkward scrutiny of strangers. It was now official: They
had filed for bankruptcy.

"You feel ashamed," Melinda says, recalling the scene in the
courtroom several years ago. "It's a blow to your ego," says
Tim. "Bankruptcy implies irresponsibility, that you couldn't

take care of your family. You don't want to be known as a failure."

But the Inmans weren't failures. Tim had started a new job as postmaster in Scottsbluff, Nebraska. Before they moved there, the Inmans had lived for seventeen years in Manhattan, Kansas, where Tim worked as a postal supervisor. Melinda homeschooled their five children and managed the household. In 1989 Tim completed his college degree while working full time.

Although he had a good job and they budgeted carefully, the cost of raising a large family put a growing strain on the Inmans' finances. Mortgage payments, groceries, upkeep on their van, the perpetual needs of the children, college loans: It all added up to less and less money at the end of each month. They debated whether Melinda should get a job, but day-care costs were prohibitive, and they were reluctant to give up homeschooling.

While seeking advice, the Inmans discovered a series of videotapes made by Christian financial counselors. These videos promised something they had never heard before: That Christians, by tithing and practicing certain other principles, could be assured of freedom from financial difficulty. The Inmans had always given money to their church, but now they began to wonder if their failure to tithe was the cause of their financial difficulties. Desiring to obey God, they began tithing.

Tim took on a second job, working on commission for a financial planning service. He and Melinda were optimistic. They had taken a step of faith, and they waited for the financial security that was promised. But almost immediately they were hit by a wave of medical expenses. Over a period of months, accidents, injuries, and other unexpected circumstances forced more than half the family members to seek medical care. The aftermath was a long list of medical bills—ambulance fees, hospital stays, bills from surgeons, anesthesiologists, physical therapists, and more. Some expenses were covered by insurance; others weren't. And even the medical care that was covered required a hefty copayment. "At one point, we were sending money to more than ten doctors and specialists," Melinda says.

At the same time, heavy rains were causing widespread flooding in their town. Water seeped up through the basement floor of their home, weakening the basement walls, which eventually buckled inward.

The Inmans were shocked and confused. After being encouraged to expect financial help from God, they had been swept into a devastating flurry of financial difficulties. The income from Tim's second job went to pay medical bills. When that wasn't enough, they started using their credit card to cover medical expenses.

Then they investigated the cost of repairing their basement. Because the house wasn't located on a flood plain, they hadn't been eligible for flood insurance. Low-interest loans were available to repair flood-damaged homes, but as work was about to begin on the Inmans' basement, new information came out concerning building code restrictions. To bring their home up to current standards, the cost of the repairs would jump from around $10,000 to nearly $40,000. What had been a difficult, but manageable, situation suddenly became a crisis. "Even with a second mortgage, our home was not worth that much," says Tim. "We couldn't qualify for a loan, and we couldn't fix the damage on our own."

Not knowing what else to do, Tim went to see an attorney. "He told me to declare bankruptcy," says Tim, "but I didn't want to do that." Another option would be to talk with the banker who had made their home loan. Perhaps the bank would forgive the debt and take the house back.

"I swallowed my pride and went to see him," Tim says. The banker was sympathetic, but he wouldn't take a house so seriously devalued by flood damage. If the Inmans turned over the house, the bank would sue them for what they still owed on their mortgage. Ten years of hard work investing in their home had vanished.

Badly shaken, they turned to Christian friends for support. Their church had offered much practical help during their medical and financial ordeals, bringing in meals and even giving them money. But Melinda and Tim sensed people withdrawing from them as they began to talk about the possibility of bankruptcy.

"It scared people," says Melinda. "We didn't fit the paradigm. We were following all the rules, and tithing, and still bad things kept happening to us."

Relentlessly, the emotional stressors multiplied. Tim's father died, which caused him to become increasingly depressed. "I forgot people's names, phone numbers, why I went to the grocery store," he says. "I didn't want to get out of bed in the morning. I'd have to walk to the back of the post office to throw up before I could start working."

Then they learned they were expecting their sixth child. Melinda knew how hard Tim was struggling, and she feels God gave her the strength to remain hopeful when everything seemed to be crumbling around them.

"Tim needed me to be optimistic, and it seemed like I was given the ability to see the good in things," she says. Melinda would point out the blessings in their lives—a son who made a deeper commitment to God, a new child on the way, the successful recovery from the many medical problems family members had faced. The Inmans also began meeting several times during the week for coffee or lunch. "We were too embarrassed to talk to anyone else," Tim says, "so we talked to each other."

But the answers weren't forthcoming. Tim felt more and more that bankruptcy might be inevitable. Melinda clung to her belief that God wouldn't allow that to happen.

When a large sales commission that Tim was counting on fell through, he and Melinda decided they had to make a change. He was selected for a postmaster's position in Nebraska, and the family moved after the birth of their daughter.

After the move, the Inmans received an offer on their house back in Kansas. "We fasted and prayed that the house would sell," says Tim.

"I begged God," Melinda says. "I don't think I've prayed for anything that hard in my life."

But the contract fell through. And the following month the Inmans filed for bankruptcy.

During their move to Nebraska, Tim spent some time alone—to recover from his depression, and to search the Bible for help. He was looking for answers to his questions about their decision to tithe and their subsequent bankruptcy. He became convinced that the advice he and Melinda had received was a one-sided portrayal of the rewards of obeying God. In fact, after he stood up in court and declared that he and

Melinda were unable to pay their debts, he felt a little more at peace.

But Melinda continued to struggle with doubts. "I thought we had failed as Christians; either God had let us down, or we had let him down," she says. Just as Tim had drawn on Melinda's optimism back in Kansas, now Melinda needed Tim's quiet assurance that God had not rejected them.

"I was lying in bed one night, and I realized I had quit talking to God," she says. "I didn't trust him anymore because I had begged him to sell our house and it didn't sell."

She confided her feelings to Tim, who continued to reassure her. She also told a friend, who encouraged her not to turn her back on God but to turn toward him and then wait. "Tell God you don't trust him anymore," the friend said. "And believe what you know about him from Scripture, even if you can't feel it right now."

Melinda joined a group that was studying the Old Testament book of Habakkuk. She found comfort in the prophet's dialogue with God, and she began to gain insight into her own struggles.

"It was hard for me to see how it could be God's will to let all those things happen—his way of refining my character and making Tim and me closer," she says. "But why should I think God can't allow bad things to happen in my life, when he allowed bad things to happen to so many people in the Old Testament? When I finally understood that, it was like a weight rolled off me."

Slowly, Melinda's optimistic faith returned. Looking back, she and Tim realize they should have researched the initial teaching they received about tithing. "We accepted a legalistic perspective, that if Christians tithed and did certain things, bad things wouldn't happen to them," says Melinda. "But we know now that we can't put God in a box. We don't make God behave in a certain way."

Having learned that giving 10 percent won't buy financial security, the Inmans sometimes feel angry about advice that glibly guarantees a prescribed response from God in exchange for obedience or trust. But they concentrate on the bigger issues, such as the overall purpose of obedience in a Christian's life. Melinda found answers in the Old Testament story of Shadrach, Meshach, and Abednego, whose choice to obey God placed their lives in jeopardy. "They trusted God, no matter how he responded," she says. "Their attitude was, 'If we die, we die.' They were determined to obey God."

Melinda and Tim now enjoy a freedom that permeates every area of their faith. Their giving is a matter between them and God, and they no longer give based on some prescription for getting something back.

Thanks to Tim's good job and the help of willing bankers, the Inmans once again own a home. And when tough times come along, their history provides a good reminder of God's nearness and support. They are convinced that financial failures don't mean God doesn't love you. "In fact," says Melinda, "this may be God's way of showing that he does love you—by bringing about the things that will conform you to the image of Christ."

Commentary

Failure can be something we do or something that happens to us. It can be something that was within our control or outside of our control. But it usually involves more than that. Failure is also an interpretation we make about what has happened. And it is that interpretation that will determine how it affects our lives.

Most of us don't understand the value of failure. We haven't learned that one of the best ways to avoid future failure is to face the present one when it occurs. We haven't learned that one of the best ways to avoid future pain is to learn from the pain we do have. We find it hard to believe that one of the best ways to minimize mistakes is to maximize the lessons we can learn from the mistakes we have already made.

Tim and Melinda are a couple who experienced financial failure. What made it especially hard is that they were good, hard-working people who were doing the best they could to do it right. They loved each other, they loved the Lord, they sought his direction in their decisions, they were committed parents, they were active in their faith, and took responsibility for their obligations.

And yet, Tim and Melinda experienced the humiliation and devastation of seeing ten years of sacrifice, hard work, and investment in their home vanish. In some ways it doesn't really matter if it was their fault or not. Bankruptcy is a blow to the ego that implies irresponsibility, incompetence, and failure. It can easily produce guilt and shame.

The Inmans made many healthy decisions along the way. While they were distressed, depressed, and discouraged, they didn't allow themselves to become puppets of their problems or slaves to their circumstances. They didn't focus on just their problems. They took some time to focus on what God was doing and where he was working. Making time to thank God, to praise him for what he is doing in the midst of circumstances and situations we don't (and may never) understand, is one of the key tools not just for *getting through*, but, even more valuable, for *growing through* a crisis.

Many couples who have experienced a significant life crisis say that one of the most helpful things they did was to apply the words of an old hymn, "Count Your Blessings." It's not as easy as it sounds but it's always more powerful than you could imagine. Melinda didn't just think about a few of her blessings. She counted them, naming them one by one.

In addition, they sought wise counsel, turned to Christian friends for support, shared their doubts and fears with each other and with those friends, and accepted some help. They spent time together, kept their communication going, and kept their sense of humor.

Tim spent some time alone to talk to God, to listen to God, to search for answers in the Bible and through prayer. Melinda joined a group. They chose to trust and obey. Through this difficult, painful, and confusing struggle they learned to redefine failure.

Tim and Melinda learned that God can use crises to get

our attention and give us an opportunity to reexamine ourselves. This can be more valuable than continuing to be safe and secure in things that are of secondary value. Failure can force us into reflection and conversation. It can help us get off the fences of life. It can push us beyond playing it safe.

Through pain, discouragement, humiliation, and suffering Melinda and Tim learned the reality of Romans 8:28-29a (NLT): "And we know that God causes everything to work together for the good of those who love God and are called according to his purpose for them. For God knew his people in advance, and he chose them to become like his Son...."

Resources

Ron Blue, *Master Your Money: A Step-by-Step Plan for Financial Freedom* (Nashville, Tenn.: Thomas Nelson, 1997).

——, *Master Your Money Workbook* (Nashville, Tenn.: Thomas Nelson, 1993).

Bill Butterworth, *When Life Doesn't Turn Out Like You Planned* (Nashville, Tenn.: Thomas Nelson, 1995).

Carole Hyatt and Linda Gottlieb, *When Smart People Fail* (New York: Viking Penguin, 1993).

Gary J. Oliver, *Made Perfect in Weakness: The Amazing Things God Can Do With Failure* (Colorado Springs, Colo.: Chariot Victor, 1995).

Chapter 3

Childhood Abuse
by Andrés Tapia

I n the fall of 1987 all our houseplants died. Their shriveled leaves announced to the world that our marriage was drying up as well. Inexplicably that summer my wife had simply lost it. I never knew what I would find when I got home.

Sometimes she would be curled up in the fetal position in a corner of our Chicago apartment, her eyes reflecting a soul drained of hope. Frightened, I'd ask her what was wrong. No answer.

Something had taken over the personality of my bride of four years, swallowing up her tenderness and laughter. Lori's mood swings were erratic, her criticism of me cutting, her terror of sex total. Our formerly happy marriage felt cursed.

As Lori grasped at remedies, it felt as if she were punching the fast forward and reverse buttons on a remote control, trying to find the right frame on a videotape. "You're distant"; "You're clingy." "You don't tell me what you're thinking"; "You talk too much." "Leave me alone"; "Don't go away." "Be more of a man"; "Your maleness frightens me."

A gifted musician, Lori stopped singing, and her piano sat silent in a corner of our home. Along with other dreams for the future, her aspirations to play the electric guitar fell away. She missed work and withdrew from her graduate school courses because she couldn't keep up. This aggravated her sense that her life was worthless, and she began talking about killing herself. She spent days unable to get out of bed.

I tried cheering her up with good news about the world, lively music, dumb jokes, tickling. My clumsy attempts only made her angrier. When I pointed out a sunshiny day, she told me, "Beautiful days are the worst." At least on gloomy days the world outside matched how she felt inside.

One dismal day when we had focused our confused anger on each other, Lori asked in a please-don't-leave-me voice, "Are you going to give up on me?" How much I wanted to say we were going to make it. But, my hope spent, I could only mumble, "I just don't know." Later Lori would capture in song how we both felt at that time: *"Bright young faces in a photograph/like flowers on their wedding day/if they knew then how hard it'd be they never would have started/The only thing that's left to do is pray."*

None of this fit what I believed about love and faith. We had been committed Christians for years. We had been friends before falling in love. We had worked through difficult issues before we got married. And we believed the Scriptures on which we'd based our lives. "Love never fails, love never fails," I repeated often as I cried myself to sleep.

But love *was* failing. Lori sought help, but she just seemed to get worse during months of therapy. Discovering that 90 percent of her symptoms matched those of people who had been sexually abused as children drove her closer to the precipice. Then her memories zeroed in on repeated abuse by a male relative outside the immediate family. The idea of someone close to her violating her body and soul made her feel as if she'd picked up the newspaper one morning and read her own obituary.

The sexual abuse of children is like psychic murder. A child's understanding of his or her place in the world is based on trust, so the betrayal mutilates the child's budding sense of self. Because a child cannot express in words what happened, the experience can get buried in the subconscious. The result is a toxic emotional system. For my wife to heal and for our love to survive, we needed nothing short of a resurrection.

The more Lori tried to deny the past sexual abuse, the more debilitated she became. And I with her. Every painful memory she pushed down disguised itself and popped up in another form, ricocheting through our marriage.

One night Lori was so paralyzed by fear of men, she couldn't even look at me. "Talk to me!" I begged, now not so much for her sake as for my own. But she withdrew even more. My soul screamed, "I'm losing her, and there's nothing I can do!" Desperate, I found myself speeding away in our car.

"Dios, tienes poder o no? God, do you have power or not?" I cried in my native Spanish. "Why do you just sit there as our marriage disintegrates?" I ended up at our pastor's house in tears. He listened, he summoned the Almighty. If Jesus could only say to me as he did to that desperate father, "Go home, for the one loved is healed." But no miracle followed. I left my pastor's home somewhat comforted but still feeling adrift.

I realized Lori wasn't the only one who needed help, but

where could I go to find answers? Our bedroom was stockpiled with books and magazine articles to guide Lori as she began to explore her past. Reading those helped me understand my wife, but I couldn't find one book to help me understand *me*. I felt insecure, guilty, and inadequate. The past abuse had ruined our sex life and driven us apart. I was throwing up because of anxiety, and I couldn't even get hold of a decent weapon to fight back with.

Lori's healing became like a second job as we juggled our schedules to include one-on-one therapy sessions as well as Lori's weekly support group meeting with other abuse survivors. One afternoon, she told me several of the women in the support group were troubled by the effect their healing processes were having on the men in their lives. I already knew some of the guys whose wives were in the group. "Maybe they are experiencing the same thing I am," I thought.

They were. It took another year for circumstances and courage to converge before four of us met over a pot of spaghetti to compare battle wounds. The four soon became five, and we were amazed at how similar our experiences were. The effect of knowing we weren't alone was powerful, immediate, and liberating.

As we shared our fears of our wives' anger or our inability to draw healthy boundaries with them, our focus unexpectedly shifted and we opened the door for God's Spirit to help us face our own struggles as men. Growing up in a home with an alcoholic mom and workaholic dad had broken me in serious ways. As I opened up with the guys over a period of weeks, strong emotions began to erupt at surprising times. One night during a prayer time with a different group of friends, a fury against my dad welled up and I slammed a friend—a brawny roofer—against a wall, yelling at him as if he were my dad: "You were never there!" We were both stunned, but my friend proceeded to pray for me.

I discovered that the way I reacted to Lori's chaos had less to do with her past than it did with my own. My terror of my wife's anger, for instance, triggered my unresolved feelings from childhood about my mother's anger. One challenging look or word from Lori about how I was, say, slicing the vegetables for supper would jolt the safe edifice I had built around my hidden turmoil.

It also became clear that Lori frequently rejected my efforts to be supportive because they were truly unhelpful. She was reacting to what I couldn't even see initially: That protecting myself was more important to me than helping her. My relationships were built around an immature attempt to make sure no one, not even Lori, got mad at me.

My pleas to God to save our marriage were partly answered by my finally accepting the basic gospel message: I can't get it together on my own; I need God's help. I had to allow others and God to help me.

In my brothers' arms, through tears, prayers, and confrontation, in tandem with professional help, I worked through emotional and spiritual issues. Like Lori, I needed to connect with past feelings, channel them appropriately, and have integrity about my current feelings. In our group, we learned—and this sounds so elementary now—to say what we felt, truthfully, yet without tearing someone else down. I left behind the days when I would stay wrapped up in unconstructive fights and eventually give in by tiptoeing around my wife, coaxing her out of being mad at me by being overly solicitous or apologizing for things that weren't my fault.

In our men's support group, we practiced better responses for those painful marital discussions and ways to distance ourselves from our wives' "acting out" behaviors. I learned to say, "Lori, you are expressing a lot of anger, but I don't think it really has to do with me. I'm going to the den to read for awhile."

During that time Lori and I attended a Los Lobos concert. Lori was being particularly prickly, for some reason. In the past I would have tensed up, tried to caress her arm, or offered to buy her a Dove bar. This time I told her I'd be back in a bit and took a walk around the outdoor concert park. When I got back I didn't fall into the oh-please-don't-be-mad-at-me routine, but instead let myself enjoy the concert. As I held my ground, Lori slowly leaned closer. Without having to "work out" her earlier prickliness, I knew we were back in sync as a couple.

As I became more able to not wilt in response to Lori's outbursts, she found it easier to face her past without fearing I would shatter. She continued moving courageously through the traditional steps of therapy. She chose to stop living as a victim and took responsibility for issues she could control—like accepting my love for her and not associating my actions with those of her abuser. As her outrage was channeled appropriately, we came to life again—emotionally, spiritually, sexually, and career-wise.

We rode out a four-year storm. Though our marriage ship had required major repairs, it was still floating and not too far off course. Soon Lori gave birth to our daughter, Marisela.

And we went on a second honeymoon to celebrate our ten-year anniversary.

There are still days when Lori's depression shows up like an unwelcome visitor. I sometimes still feel panic begin to rise inside me. But now Lori and I, with God's help, fight it out within ourselves or with each other—and move on.

Today our home is alive again with Lori's music. As distortion blares out of her Peavey amp, I'm partly listening, partly playing with Marisela, and partly brainstorming article ideas over a small scrap of paper. I momentarily stop what I'm doing to marvel at the sound of resurrected life in our home—Lori's soulful voice riding the hard-edged wail of her electric guitar.

Commentary

What a shock to be married for four years to a tender, happy, fun-loving wife and suddenly discover that the woman you love and think you know has left and another person has taken her place—the same body but a different personality. You try everything you can to make her feel better. It doesn't matter what you try, things just get worse.

Obviously this couple had done many things right. They had laid a good foundation for their marriage. They had been friends before falling in love, they loved the Lord, they believed the Bible, and still everything around them appeared to be falling apart. Does it sound impossible? Unbelievable? Well, believe it or not, the experience of Lori and Andrés is not that uncommon for someone who has been sexually abused. Andrés is correct when he states, "The sexual abuse of children is like psychic murder."

It can stay hidden for awhile but, as Dr. Dan Allender observes, "Sexual abuse doesn't devastate only a victim's internal world. Whatever damage is done internally will eventually affect the external, observable life" (*The Wounded Heart*, 157). The first response of the victim is often to deny that anything has happened. However, most victims' experiences are the same as Lori's: the more they deny things, the worse the symptoms get. Their husbands try to help but the help doesn't work. Many men become confused, reactive, and defensive. Their emotions over their wives' experiences bring out some of their own issues.

There are several very positive things that Lori and Andrés did. First of all, they got some information. In this step Andrés discovered that 90 percent of Lori's symptoms matched those of someone who had been sexually abused. Sexual abuse involves secondary symptoms that usually are what draw a victim to reach out for help. These symptoms include physical complaints, eating disorders, self-destructiveness, low self-esteem, depression, addictions and compulsions, and sexual dysfunction.

Next, they reached out for spiritual and psychological help. Andrés went to his pastor. He cried out in prayer to God. While he didn't hear a voice from heaven, he continued to pray. At the risk of sounding like I'm spiritualizing, I can say that after forty years as a Christian and thirty years as a counselor and psychologist, prayer is the least understood and most underutilized tool in the healing process. Abraham Herschel writes:

> Prayer is not a stratagem for occasional use, a refuge to resort to now and then. It is rather like an established residence for the innermost self. All things have a home; the bird has a nest, the fox has a hole, the bee has a hive. A soul without prayer is a soul without a home.
>
> Abraham Joshua Herschel in *Moral Grandeur and Spiritual Audacity*, quoted in *Christiantity Today* (April 27, 1998), 93

Lori became involved in a support group and sought support from others in a similar situation. She and Andrés continued to read. Many men make the mistake of thinking, "This is just about my wife." Wrong! Gradually Andrés realized that Lori wasn't the only one who needed help. One of the principles of spiritual growth is that God often uses our spouses' stuff to help us deal with our own stuff.

As Andrés learned how to understand and deal with his own emotions, he was in a better place to help Lori. As he had the courage to risk sharing his emotions with other men he became aware of what he needed to change. With information, inspiration, and support he became able to respond out of strength rather than react out of weakness. As he became stronger, Lori felt safer.

They did more than "ride out" their four-year storm. They learned more about their emotions—what they are and where they come from. They discovered that strong emotions may emerge at surprising times. They each took responsibility for their destructive behaviors from the past. They stayed committed. They learned to speak the truth in love.

They didn't quit. They learned that healing, growth, and maturity take time. There are times in life when our agonized questions don't find any satisfactory answers, when nothing we do makes any difference in our situation, when the situation is past our ability to manage it and we're not sure how we will be able to endure any more. Yet, somehow, from somewhere, we find the strength to take the next step, to hope against hope that God's promises really are true and that, although it seems impossible and feels hopeless, there is enough hope and help to at least stand.

Paul writes, "And after you have done everything ... stand" (Eph 6:13). Paul learned, Andrés and Lori learned, and the other couples whose stories are contained in this book learned that there are times in life when just standing is success. Refusing to be pushed over. You may not be going ahead, but you are not being pushed back either. You may wobble back and forth for awhile. But you are standing. Lori and Andrés discovered, and you will discover, that after you've stood for awhile, wobbled a bit, perhaps lost your footing once or twice, you'll be able to take that first small step forward. That's growth. That's maturity. That's the path to victorious Christian living.

Resources

Dan B. Allender, *The Wounded Heart* (Colorado Springs, Colo.: NavPress, 1990).

——, *The Wounded Heart Workbook* (Colorado Springs, Colo.: NavPress, 1992).

Mike Flynn, *The Mustard Seed Book: Growing Faith in Your Own Backyard* (Grand Rapids, Mich.: Chosen, 1995).

Don and Jan Frank, *When Victims Marry: Building a Stronger Marriage by Breaking Destructive Cycles* (San Bernardino, Calif.: Here's Life Publishers, 1990).

Jan Frank, *A Door of Hope: Recognizing and Resolving the Pains of Your Past* (San Bernardino, Calif.: Here's Life Publishers, 1987).

Gary J. Oliver, *Real Men Have Feelings Too* (Chicago: Moody Press, 1993).

Gary J. Oliver and H. Norman Wright, *Good Women Get Angry* (Ann Arbor, Mich.: Servant, 1995).

Chapter 4

Unemployment
by Gregg Lewis

V *ic Glavach received word the week he and Betsey returned home after the funeral of Betsey's father. It was one of those "mutually agreed upon" decisions. No devastating pink slip. No angry letter of resignation. Vic, a vice-president of development at a college in the Northeast, would leave his position immediately, though he would have help with the transition. The college would assist him for a time while he searched for another position.*

It was as amicable as such things can be. And yet, for the first time in his adult life, Vic was without a job—with no idea in the world what he would do next.

Vic: I've talked to many people who felt devastated when they lost their jobs. But I felt pretty optimistic to start with. I'd never had any trouble getting a job; I had a network of great contacts across the country. I actually felt excited about the possibility of trying something new. Maybe we'd even be able to move back to Florida where we had lived before.

I sent out more than six hundred personalized letters to organizations and individuals I knew. I made phone calls and followed up every reasonable lead. As time passed and I saw less and less fruit from my search, my discouragement grew.

Betsey: During the weeks before Vic's vacation pay ran out, I had no appetite, I lost weight. I took a part-time job that gave me something to concentrate on during the week. But I'd fall apart every weekend and cry off and on for two days. I knew it was irrational: We were two educated, talented, able-bodied people. We would find work. But it seemed like my worst nightmare had come true. In fact, I remember the day I was lying down, trying to rest, when I had this vivid mental image of my head rolling off my body and my arms just falling off. It didn't take much to interpret that imagery: I felt as if I were coming apart. And it scared me.

I think the fact that we'd each lost a parent in the preceding year helped prepare us for this experience. We'd become sensitive to each other's feelings and cycles of emotion. We had shared those hurts and learned to depend on each other in a new way. And we needed all we'd learned.

Vic: When I was down Betsey helped pull me up and when she was down I'd do the same for her. She'd be fine all week while I was getting more and more discouraged with all the negative results of my search. Her encouragement would keep me going. Then I'd feel positive enough to encourage her when she hit bottom on the weekends.

When the Glavaches decided to put their house on the market, they learned the real estate market had been dropping. The best they could hope for would be to break even when they sold it.

When it didn't sell, Vic and Betsey had new decisions to make. None of their prayers seemed to be answered. The optimism they had felt was fast eroding to despair.

Betsey: The first time Vic became depressed it terrified me. I thought, "What if he doesn't come out of this? What can I do to bring him out of it?"

I eventually learned to accept the low points as natural. I could let him have a low day or two—telling myself that I'd begin to worry if it got to a week. It never did.

But the fear was horrendous. *What if....* You have to learn to calm that fear as you go.

I think one thing that helped me was that from the very start I determined that I was not going to let this experience destroy our marriage. As much as possible I tried to separate this experience from our relationship. When Vic became discouraged, I would remind him of all the things he'd accomplished in the past.

Vic: I think we learned that marriage is really a symbiotic relationship. We need to be there for each other. And Betsey was certainly there for me. She'd tell me I could do anything. She'd remind me of the things I'd done well in the past.

Betsey: Also, I think we both came to a deeper appreciation for sex because we saw it was a real gift we had for each other. It served as an escape and helped hold us together. It reminded us that something in life was still wonderful by allowing us times to forget the troubles and just experience joy.

Vic: One night we were lying in bed when I started crying like a baby. Betsey didn't break down. She just held on and encouraged me. She proved I could depend on her—even at my lowest point.

The Glavaches faced a lot of low points as the months rolled past. Little signs of encouragement and hope kept them going. Always there seemed to be one more job lead that sounded good. But each time new hope was dashed, the resulting lows seemed to grow deeper and deeper.

Betsey: The lowest point was probably the second summer of Vic's unemployment. When I tried to imagine what I could do to escape, the only escape I could see was divorcing Vic and getting away from it all. Though I never let go of my determination not to let the experience destroy our marriage, still the thought was there.

Whenever the pain began to feel unbearable, my only defense was to stop trying to think about escaping it and just feel it. I just let the pain roll over me like ocean waves, and realized they weren't going to destroy me.

My parents were missionaries. I've been a Christian since childhood. And because I'd never really run into anything in my life for which I didn't have a pretty easy answer, I had these little neat boxes in my mind about how God worked and how he answered prayer.

We prayed so much. And when things went so long without

a positive answer, I went through a painful process of questioning the beliefs I'd held all my life. What if none of it was true?

Those doubts were fleeting. But they were still devastating to someone who believed what I had believed all my life. How could I doubt God?

When I got beyond the negative emotions and could see things rationally, I found it was easier to believe in a creative, loving God than it was to discard my beliefs. And I was able to look back and see God's care, his provision, and his timing in many of the things that happened during our ordeal.

Several weeks after Vic's last regular paycheck, he got a consulting job, a fund-raising project that carried us over Christmas and into the next year. And shortly after that, a friend from church offered Vic a job at his company installing locks. So in the year and a half Vic searched for a job, there were fewer than four months when he didn't have *some* source of income. It wasn't as much money as he had been making before, but there was always just enough to pay each week's bills.

Vic: About fifteen months into my search, I had an appointment in another state I felt good about. They had accepted more than 160 applications and had narrowed the list down to six. I was on that list.

I thought the interview went well. By the time I reached home, a letter had already arrived. Basically it said "Sorry, you're not the person we wanted for the job." I just sank into a chair, utterly defeated. In the few days that followed, I took a long look at my goals and at my relationship with God. It isn't that I had lost my faith, but I reevaluated the "you scratch my back and I'll scratch yours" attitude we tend to get into with God when we experience difficult times.

Going to the unemployment office was a memorable experience. It's a humbling thing. The ground is level in the unemployment line. You're standing there with laborers, salesmen, teachers. The fact that you used to be a college vice-president doesn't cut it. Some people come in suits, carrying briefcases, while others wear grubby, dirty clothes. You know most of them feel like you do, embarrassed to be there but grateful there's a system like it. Even though the check I received was only a fifth of what my salary had been, I needed that money to put bread on the table during the two months when I didn't have any other income.

The whole out-of-work experience forced me to accept a reality most of us have to wrestle with in middle age: Chances are, we're not going to be some important name in history. But if we're not going to change the world, maybe we need to concentrate on a small part of it. I can make a difference with my family, my neighbors, and my friends. That thought gave me something to focus on.

Both Betsey and Vic cite the maturity and support of their children as a great help in coping with their ongoing family crisis. Gigi and Landy found part-time jobs. Fourteen-year-old Danny earned money to buy the equipment he needed to go out for hockey. Going into the second summer of the job search, Gigi volunteered to sit out her final term in college if that would make it possible for Landy to begin his freshman year on schedule. Vic and Betsey weren't sure there would be tuition for anyone.

Vic: Gigi would call from college regularly to ask how I was doing. Our sons always wanted to know what was in the works. They prayed for me and encouraged me.

Betsey: When Vic lost his job, I didn't feel we had a real support group. We'd lived in the area only a couple of years and didn't have a lot of close friends. But a few months into our search I was praying and pleading with God to open a door that would give some sign of his love and concern. About a half-hour later the phone rang. Some people from our church were calling to invite us to join their small group Bible study; they wanted us to come to a potluck supper that very evening. We went and that small group became our support group. Those friends cared for us, prayed with us, and gave us a place to share our concerns and our feelings.

Many friends who called or wrote to express their caring and interest encouraged me, especially those who'd been through similar situations. Those people gave us the gift of hope. You don't realize how important hope is until you go through tough times.

And then there were the friends who sent money. It was so moving to realize people had that kind of commitment and concern.

Vic: I don't know if you can ever get used to receiving unsolicited gifts from generous friends. That, too, is humbling.

We kept a list of all the gifts we received and intend to pay them all back when we're able. If someone doesn't want to be paid back I plan to tell them to use the money to do for someone else what they did for us.

If there's any advice I would give to people who have friends and acquaintances out of work it's that you need to do more than hand out what one friend calls "non-negotiable God-bless-you's." As Christians we need to do more than say, "I'll pray for you." We need to refer them to new leads, introduce them to someone who might help, take them out, give them money. By being practical we give people hope.

Betsey: We had some good friends who regularly invited us to go sailing with them. It gave us a chance to forget the drudgery of the job search for a day or an afternoon. It wouldn't have to be sailing; it could be something as simple as a picnic that gives you a chance to experience normal life and normal pleasures.

Also, when a couple goes through something like we have, you have to focus on the positive things that happen. It helped me to set my mind on the end of the ordeal. I kept telling myself it would someday end.

I'd also recommend reading the Psalms. They come alive in difficult times when you realize thousands of years ago a writer had the exact feelings you're having right now.

You need to learn to live on other people's joy. By that I mean you need to take encouragement from other people's stories of struggle and overcoming. And look for all the ways you can find to be encouraging and supportive of each other.

Vic: For wives in situations like we went through I have several suggestions. Find a friend you can confide in and from whom you can get wisdom and strength; Betsey found an older woman she could confide in so she wasn't totally dependent on me for all her support.

Realize you can have a direct effect on the ability of your husband to find a job. Your encouragement can make all the difference.

There's a tendency in any crisis situation to place demands on your partner. Instead, look for ways to make your spouse happy.

Get out together as a couple with other couples.

For men in my situation I'd add: Spend the necessary money to find a job. Don't be afraid to run up your phone bill. Take whatever opportunities you have to get out of the house. Develop a daily routine. And take care of yourself physically.

Find something you're good at and spend time doing it. It'll help your self-esteem.

Be willing to swallow your pride and do what you need to do to put food on the table. I took a job—wearing a second-hand uniform that said my name was "Arty"—installing locks for a starting pay of eight dollars an hour. I found I enjoyed working with my hands and I had the satisfaction of knowing I was earning money we needed.

Finally, I'd encourage people to remember that in spite of the struggle and the fact that an experience like ours can bring a tremendous sense of failure, it can also strengthen you and your marriage relationship. It did for us.

After his second summer of unemployment, Vic accepted a position as director of development with a Midwest-based foundation. The Glavaches are renting out their East Coast house.

Commentary

Unemployment, especially for long periods of time, produces a myriad of confusing and conflicting emotions for both husbands and wives, and has destructive effects on relationships. One of the core emotions that emerges is fear. Men and women share many of the same fears but some significant differences exist in the kinds of things that cause them fear. Women's fears are more likely to revolve around relationships, isolation, loss of love, and abandonment. They don't have this overpowering need to appear brave or courageous or invincible. Their identity is not as much in what they do, but much more in who they are and in their relationships.

Men are more likely to fear anything that robs them of their power and control, anything that might make them look less like a man. Typically this means they avoid anything that shows weakness, failure, or lack of courage. The average man can handle physically threatening situations. But if you want to make him feel weak, vulnerable, and less secure you only have to raise doubts about his strength, stature, or ability to provide. Most men are likely to feel threatened and become discouraged when they sense criticism, condemnation, disapproval, rejection, humiliation, or exposure of their weaknesses.

Throughout the process, Vic and Betsey made many healthy decisions. In some ways, their story could be a textbook for how to face unemployment. In the beginning they were optimistic: Vic initiated a job search with a thorough plan that involved six hundred personalized letters to organizations and individuals. He was expressive of his feelings, so Betsey was able to monitor what was going on within him; he was able to express weakness and shed tears.

Betsey showed a great deal of wisdom and self-control when she chose to minimize her criticism of Vic. As a couple they helped each other: When one was down the other was up, they maintained a physical relationship that provided an escape, a source of strength, a sense that they were not alone. They reached out to the Lord and to their friends; they weren't too proud to receive help and encouragement from others.

As weeks turned into months and the hours and hours of hard work didn't seem to make any difference, Vic faced the inevitable wall of disappointment, discouragement, and despair. At this point it would have been easy for him to become problem-focused and allow his situation to determine his reality.

So much of what Vic and Betsey experienced is normal. For Betsey the loss of appetite, the weight loss, the emotional roller coaster including falling apart on weekends was all part of the process. As time went on and the energy wore thin it was easy for decision making to become impaired. As stress built and depression increased, Vic even entertained the thought that maybe it was time for his life to be over. However, in the midst of the depression another wise decision was made. Betsey recalls, "I determined that I was not going to let this experience destroy our marriage." She decided that they were going to get up one time more than they had fallen down.

Several years ago I heard Robert Schuller say, "Success is a matter of not quitting and failure is a matter of giving up too soon." At times I have looked back and thought, "If only I had kept at it. If only I had tried one more time. Might I have succeeded?" Sometimes we have set unrealistic goals or the events of life that are beyond our control are such that the best choice is to quit. However, there are times when failure is caused by simply giving up too soon.

Being educated, talented, able-bodied Christians won't keep us from the kinds of experiences where our answers don't seem to work, where all the verses we've memorized seem to fall short of the reality of the fear and pain. It won't prevent situations that cause us to question the things we've believed all of our lives. If you are in a similar situation I'd encourage you to follow the recipe that Vic and Betsey used. Pray together, find a small group to be a part of, intentionally encourage each other, seek wise counsel, let your friends help you, focus on the positive things (Phil 4:8), read the Psalms (Ps 40:1-3 is a great place to start), find a friend you can trust, develop a daily routine including exercise, and remember that the process may take time.

Resources

Bill Butterworth, *When Life Doesn't Turn Out Like You Planned* (Nashville, Tenn.: Thomas Nelson, 1995).

Ray Pritchard, *Keep Believing: God in the Midst of Our Deepest Struggles* (Chicago: Moody Press, 1997).

Jan and David Stoop, *Saying Good-Bye to Disappointments: Finding Hope When Your Dreams Don't Come True* (Nashville, Tenn.: Thomas Nelson, 1993).

John Trent, *Life Mapping* (Colorado Springs, Colo.: Focus on the Family, 1994).

Chapter 5

Death of a Child
by Gregg Lewis

*F*rom the time they were married, the Shewans' marriage seemed blessed. They were very happy together. Bill, as executive director of North Central Indiana Youth for Christ, headed a successful, growing evangelistic ministry to young people in eleven high schools and junior highs. He also served in a variety of regional and national Youth for Christ posts.

Michelle had a half-time job on a college campus that utilized her graduate training in counseling and psychology. They had recently bought an old house in a beautiful tree-lined neighborhood and had begun a series of ambitious remodeling plans. Their firstborn son, three-year-old William "Beau" Shewan IV, was a focal point of their busy lives, making friends of all ages in the neighborhood and charming people wherever his parents took him. And they proudly took him everywhere.

Friends would smile, shake their heads, and say, "Everything always seems to work out for Michelle and Bill." Their marriage, their careers, their family: Everything was under control and *running according to plan—until life began to unravel in ways that threatened their sanity, their faith, and their marriage.*

Bill: It began early in the summer of 1986. My two full-time staff people, on whom I depended to help oversee our large volunteer staff, were moving on to other jobs. Their replacements couldn't begin until fall. About the same time, my secretary resigned. I was suddenly all alone with a million details to be handled for the upcoming year.

My three-year-old son, Beau, had eye surgery in June. And while it was fairly routine it proved extremely stressful to us.

Then a few weeks later Michelle gave birth to twins, and life was suddenly and completely out of control.

Michelle: The first couple of months we survived on adrenaline and the excitement and newness of the babies. Summer is a slower time for Bill, so he could be home to help more.

By fall, about the time Bill always gets swamped in beginning-of-the-school-year details, the lack of sleep was beginning to take its toll. I was exhausted by the effort to establish a manageable routine, nurse the twins, and care for Bill and Beau. I'd so enjoyed the intimacy I'd had with Beau as a baby, but I quickly realized there was no way to have the same kind of individual time with Jessica and Jay.

Bill: Michelle recruited friends to come and help when I was gone, but the parade of helpers sometimes made for more stress.

I wanted to help ease the load, but I couldn't do enough. There just never seemed to be any free time or energy. Every night we went to bed knowing we'd be up four or five times in the night.

Through it all I tried to put a good face on the situation, reminding myself as well as Michelle: "This is just a stage. Life won't always be like this."

Michelle: I crashed physically with the flu in October. The kids were sick too. And since I didn't have the stamina to keep nursing, I weaned Jay. But I wasn't really ready for that and neither was Jay.

I felt bad that I couldn't be supportive of Bill; on the other hand I resented the fact that I felt as if I were going down the tubes and he wasn't saving me.

Bill: In December, I came to a difficult decision. I resigned from all my regional and national responsibilities. It was hard to give them up.

In addition to my increased time at home, we hired one consistent baby-sitter to help Michelle several times during the week. That gave us, Beau, and the twins a sense of stability we didn't have with the constantly changing guard of volunteers. And in what may have been the most hopeful development of all, Jessica and Jay finally seemed to be getting their schedules in sync, and even began to sleep through some nights. The worst seemed to be over.

Michelle: Bill's being home more and the other changes he mentioned should have taken off the pressure. They did help, and life seemed better. But I was worse. All the frustration and disappointment of the past seven months were still there; I still wasn't doing the job I wanted to do as a mother.

Many nights I hardly slept at all. During the days I was a zombie. Finally, in February, there were three nights in a row that I didn't sleep. By the fourth night I was scared. I was teetering on the edge of a precipice. I knew I had to get help. The next morning, with Bill's blessing, I made an appointment with a psychiatrist at the county mental health center.

The doctor not only seemed to understand my feelings of disappointment and stress, but he diagnosed my depression and pinpointed the event that had triggered it—weaning Jay back in the fall when we'd all been so sick. I knew immediately the doctor was right.

He also prescribed an antidepressant. He explained that the long months of stress had destroyed the chemical balance in my body, and that the chemical that enabled the nervous system to shut down in sleep was no longer strong enough to do its job. "If you don't take this," he said, "you're going to end up in a hospital very soon." So I took it. I also began to see a counselor.

March was a good month. After only a few sessions, I felt ready to give up the counseling. I felt physically and emotionally able to cope again. Life no longer felt like an eternal treadmill. I had energy to give again. And there was even time to spend with Beau, like the day I got a big appliance box and let him cover it with remnants of wallpaper. I was a mother again. I had felt guilty about how little time I'd had for him since the twins were born.

Bill: I took Beau with me for a week-long spring break trip to Florida with a busload of teenagers. Michelle invited her mother to stay with her and the twins while Beau and I were gone.

He got a little homesick for the first couple of days, but for the most part he was his usual fun-loving self. He got a big kick out of squirting the high school kids with his water pistol.

At a big waterslide park, Beau started to experience severe stomach cramps. The park had a nurse on duty. She said the symptoms sounded like a flu virus that was going around. Since the camp director's kids and our guest speaker's kids had had the flu, I felt certain Beau had caught the bug. But the rest of the day he alternated between severe pain and short naps due to exhaustion from the cramps.

At one point when he was awake and fussing, we called home from the water park so Beau could talk to Michelle and get a little long-distance mother love. Concerned about Beau, Michelle wondered if he was having an appendicitis attack. I told her the nurse had ruled that out and assured her it was just the flu and that everything would be all right. The phone call helped, and I reminded Beau that the trip was more than half over and we'd be starting home in a couple of days.

Late in the afternoon he began vomiting. So when we got back to the camp that evening I took him right to the motel-like room he and I shared and put him in bed. He threw up several times, so I forced him to drink liquids to keep him from getting dehydrated. But he couldn't keep anything down. We slept in the same bed that night, with me stroking his head and rubbing his back when he'd begin to cry about his stomach cramps. At one point he said to me, "I sure am sick."

Thursday morning came and went. That afternoon, when he threw up what looked like blood, I decided to get medical help. The doctor we saw did a litmus-type test of Beau's saliva and determined he had indeed thrown up some blood. He said it wasn't uncommon for young children with a violent flu to rupture a small blood vessel. Throwing up a little blood was consistent with the other flu symptoms. Beau didn't have a bad fever and the doctor used his stethoscope to listen to the reassuring gurgling sounds of Beau's intestines. The symptoms were consistent with the flu that was making the rounds. So the doctor gave me some medicine to suppress the vomiting and advised me to keep giving him liquids.

I took Beau back to our room at camp. But as the afternoon went on, he didn't seem to be getting any better. The camp director came to check on us about eight that evening. When he heard Beau crying and beginning to complain about his legs hurting, the director left to call his family's pediatrician.

Moments after the director left us, Beau began complaining about his arms hurting as well. A few minutes later he flopped over on his back with his limbs outstretched and exclaimed, "Don't touch me!" Then he began motioning frantically with one hand toward his face.

"Are you going to throw up?" I asked. He shook his head no.

"You want a drink?" Again, no.

Suddenly I realized what was happening. He was gasping for air. His body wasn't getting any oxygen. And I knew I was losing him.

I screamed, "Oh God, don't let him die! Please don't let him die!" As my voice echoed off the walls of the room I suddenly stopped screaming out of embarrassment that came with the irrational thought, "What if someone hears me?"

But the next minute Beau's eyes rolled back in his head and his body went limp. The terror surged inside me again and once more I screamed, "No! Please, God, don't let him die!"

I put my ear to his chest and thought I could detect a very faint heartbeat, so I quickly began administering cardiopulmonary resuscitation (CPR). I don't know how long it was, probably only minutes, before one of the other staff people arrived to check on us and began helping me with the CPR. Paramedics arrived within minutes and took over. While they worked over Beau, those of us in the room prayed for him. The others were saying, "Don't give up hope," but I knew it was too late.

Since we were a thirty-minute drive from the hospital in Gainesville, Florida, the paramedics called for a helicopter to speed Beau to the emergency room. The camp director drove me to Gainesville, and I prayed as we raced through the darkness. When I walked into the hospital the doctors confirmed what I already knew in my heart. Beau had been declared dead on arrival.

I knew I had to call Michelle. I wanted just the right words to soften the blow, but there were no such words. I dialed. I heard the phone ring. Michelle answered.

"Hi," I said. "How are you doing?"

"We're all fine," she said. "How's Beau? Is he better?"

I still didn't know what to say. So I said the first words that came to mind: "Beau's gone to be with the Lord."

Michelle began screaming. I heard her mother in the background asking, "What's wrong? What's wrong?" Michelle choked out the words, "Beau died." And then I heard my mother-in-law scream as Michelle wept hysterically. I could do nothing but hold the receiver and listen helplessly to my wife crying more than a thousand miles away. That and cry with her.

Michelle: I couldn't believe it. I'd talked to Beau at the water park just the day before. Now he was dead? How was it possible? I don't know how long it was before I got control enough to ask, "What happened?"

All Bill could say was a feeble, "I don't know." The doctor he had talked to hadn't known either. Bill quickly, painfully, recounted what had happened, but I don't know that any of the details really sank in before he was called away from the phone.

I remember the minute he hung up I prayed, "O God, please let it be something bizarre that caused Beau's death so there isn't any way I can blame Bill." I was afraid if it turned out there was something Bill could have done, I'd blame him. It could even destroy our marriage.

Bill: Flying home alone was pure hell. No one yet had any explanations, so I was tormented by the fear that I'd done something wrong or that I should have done something else.

I sat in the cabin of that airplane with a fire raging in my throat, knowing I couldn't cry out loud in the midst of all those other passengers, just hoping I could make it home without losing it.

But by the time my folks and Michelle met me at the airport and I took Michelle in my arms, I couldn't even cry. I think shock had set in. The next few days were a blur. We carefully planned the funeral service to be a positive testimony of our faith in God.

Michelle: We both had enough counseling experience to expect tough times ahead. But the funeral director, who was a personal friend, gave us some literature written for parents who lose a child, and what we read scared us. Some researchers say 80 percent of all marriages fail within five years of a child's death. Others put the figure around 50 percent in the first year. What is undeniable is that the death of a child can be a serious threat to the stability of any marriage.

Bill: What we read warned that most of the problems revolved around two common issues—either guilt and blame or differences in the grieving process between the two spouses.

Fortunately we had little reason to struggle with guilt or blame. The autopsy revealed that Beau had died of a rare condition—intussusception—which is almost unheard of in children over two years of age. (Beau was almost four.) Part of his small intestine had telescoped into his large intestine to create a blockage. Food couldn't go anywhere, thus the vomiting. Beau's body quickly began using up its supply of electrolytes that keep the body's systems running. The kidneys and liver weren't doing their job, so poison spread quickly through Beau's body. His lungs had filled with fluid, and when he died it was the result of massive system failure and there was no way to stop it. The pediatric pathologist at the hospital in Florida said it was doubtful they could have saved Beau even had the problem been diagnosed hours earlier. He didn't think they would have been able to stabilize him enough to survive emergency intestinal surgery.

What made it even more impossible to impute human blame was the fact that Beau never exhibited the classic symptoms of intussusception. He had no fever. The doctor had heard the sounds of digestion. Beau should have passed out from the pain. No one could have known. In fact, Beau's case was so unusual that it is destined to be used as a case study of intussusception that failed to present itself in any of its classic ways.

But while we never had to wrestle with guilt or try to blame each other for Beau's death, Michelle and I did realize that the differences in the way we would grieve could create a barrier between us.

Michelle: So we made the joint decision early in our grieving process to always be willing to talk when one or the other of us felt like talking about Beau. Even so, we were aware that we were each struggling differently with our responses to Beau's death. No matter how much it helped to talk to each other, we needed other perspectives. So we decided to go for counseling, to the same therapist but for different sessions. Some of the differences in our grief became more evident in the issues we discussed with the counselor.

Part of what I struggled with was the fact that I no longer wanted to parent and I still had two active nine-month-olds who needed more from me than I wanted to give. In my therapy I had to wrestle with the realization that I was in a sort of self-imposed holding pattern—just marking time, waiting for my own life to be over so I could see Beau again. I knew that wasn't healthy. But it seemed all I could handle emotionally was to get up each morning, walk through the motions of the day, and climb back into bed at night.

And then there was the guilt that hit me every time I stopped to realize that life really was easier with only two children to care for. I remembered wishing I had only two instead of three. I never believed that I had willed Beau's death, but the memory of those old thoughts and questions grieved me.

Bill: I struggled a lot with the question of where to channel my anger. I couldn't feel comfortable being angry with God. I worked hard at not displacing my anger toward Michelle. But it wasn't satisfying being angry with a circumstance or even being angry with Satan over a messed-up world.

Michelle: We both felt so vulnerable. I'd always tried to trust God for the smallest details of my life. But what could I trust him for now, after he'd failed to protect something as important to me as the life of my own son? I sensed God's presence and grace were still in my life, but I wanted more than that. I wanted to be able to trust him again. And I didn't know if I ever could. I felt so helpless, so vulnerable. What was to say the twins wouldn't die, too?

Bill: We had suddenly become fearful people. Every time one of the twins coughed, we jumped. Night after night I had horrible dreams about children dying gory deaths. And during the day I feared for my continued ministry because I remembered a pastor I'd known who walked away from the church in despair after the death of his son. And I wasn't sure how, or if, I'd be able to function in my job when another school year began.

The summer was tough. Everywhere we turned there were painful reminders of Beau. His toys remained around the house because the twins were beginning to play with them. Every time I walked in the back door at the end of the day without having him come running to greet me was another reminder.

And as determinedly as we tried to face our grief together, so much of what Michelle and I felt was individual and personal. There were times we couldn't seem to help but pull away. I remember telling Michelle one night, "It's not that I don't love you anymore, I just don't have anything to give you."

Michelle: When school did start again, Bill found the strength to go on. He realized that he could trust God again. I resented the progress I saw him making. And I was angry that after all those months of stress and depression the year before, now I had to be working through long months of grief.

After a year, Bill and I still sometimes cried together, but those tears were coming less frequently. I think our marriage is stronger than ever now—but for the longest time we were still at different stages of grief.

Bill: We have learned valuable lessons, including the recognition that despite our individual efforts, this world is an out-of-control mess. When life comes crashing down on a marriage, all you can do is trust God and hang on to each other. That's the only hope we've got, but it's enough.

Commentary

Sometimes a crisis hits like a bolt of lightning out of the blue. At other times the events of our lives seem to slowly deteriorate and the cumulative effect is to wear us down and make us more vulnerable to a crisis. That's what happened to Bill and Michelle. As their story begins they are a normal, healthy couple whose desire is to serve Jesus and be a good mom and dad. They have the normal stress and pressure of a normal couple living in a fallen world. Then events begin to mount that increase their stress.

I sometimes refer to having preschoolers as the twilight zone of marriage. It is a very special time for parents, but it is also a time of enormous stress, pressure, lack of sleep, and readjustments. Bill and Michelle had three preschoolers. No wonder they write that "life was suddenly and completely out of control."

It's no surprise that Michelle began to experience the symptoms of depression. What surprised me was that it didn't happen sooner. It is unfortunate that some Christians find it hard to admit that they experience depression.

Depression produces changes in how our body functions, how we emotionally feel, and how we think. Depression is an emotion. But when we allow it to consume our lives it becomes more than an emotion. It can become a way of life. It must be identified and dealt with. Michelle and Bill had the wisdom to see a counselor. Fortunately, this person understood depression and understood that there was a biochemical component to her depression. Depression almost always has more than one cause, and often there is a physiological factor involved. Fortunately there are a number of safe and effective antidepressants available. When prescribed appropriately, antidepressant medications such as Prozac, Zoloft, and Celexa can be of great value in restoring the God-designed functioning of neurotransmitters in our central nervous system that affect and regulate mood.

The story could have ended here and been a dramatic example of the cumulative effects of stress on marriages and families. I wish the story had ended at this point. But it didn't. The loss of a loved one is painful. The loss of a child is devastating. The sudden loss of a child compounds the devastation. In *Grief Counseling and Grief Therapy*, William Wordon identifies seven specific features that tend to complicate the grief process for survivors of a sudden-death experience:

1. Sudden death usually leaves the survivor with a sense of unreality that may last a long time.
2. Sudden death fosters a stronger-than-normal sense of guilt expressed in "if only ..." statements.
3. In sudden death, the need to blame someone for what happened is extremely strong.
4. Sudden death often involves medical and legal authorities.
5. Sudden death often elicits a sense of helplessness on the part of the survivor.

6. Sudden death leaves the survivor with many regrets and a sense of unfinished business.

7. In the event of a sudden death, there is the need to understand why it happened. Along with this is the need to ascribe not only the cause but the blame. Sometimes God is the only available target and it is not uncommon to hear someone say, "I hate God."

The question isn't, "Is there life after loss?" The real question is, "What quality of life can there be after loss?" You can't always control the losses in your life. You can control the kind of person you become because of those losses!

The are several facts about grief that are important to remember. The only way out of grief is through it. Grieving is hard work. Effective grief work is not done alone. Bill and Michelle did many good things. First of all they reached out to God, to some friends, and to a professional counselor. Grief is a process, and when you understand what is normal and healthy it is easier to move through the potential relational minefield in ways that help and heal.

They allowed themselves to experience and express their God-given emotions. They reached out to friends. Bill communicated his anger. They maintained good communication and made a joint decision early in the grieving process to always be willing to talk when one or the other of them felt like talking about Beau. They acknowledged that the grieving process is different for different people and each allowed the other the freedom to grieve in his or her own way. Many couples have found it helpful to join a support group for parents who have lost children.

I'm grateful to Bill and Michelle for their courage and their candor. They are a testimony to the fact that God can use the losses of our lives to help deepen our character and increase our maturity. Their example as well as the clear teaching of Scripture confirms the fact that character traits such as humility, endurance, patience, long-suffering, gratitude, and self-control grow out of how we choose to respond to our losses.

Resources

Bob Deits, *Life After Loss: A Personal Guide Dealing with Death, Divorce, Job Change, and Relocation* (Tucson, Ariz.: Fisher, 1992).

Raymond R. Mitsch and Lynn Brookside, *Grieving the Loss of Someone You Love* (Ann Arbor, Mich.: Servant, 1993).

H. Norman Wright, *Recovering from the Losses of Life* (Tarrytown, N.Y.: Revell, 1991).

Chapter 6

Workaholism
by Janis Long Harris

When the phone rang, Bev Tindall was alone in the apartment, completely unprepared for her husband's words. "I'm sorry, honey," Gene said softly, "but I'm not coming back home. I just can't do it."

Bev stood by the phone in shock. She and Gene had come back to the United States from their mission post in Venezuela in order to work on their troubled marriage. Bev had come back first, seeking help for the "nerves" that sometimes left her so depressed that she could barely get out of bed in the morning. Then mission officials sent for Gene, who reluctantly flew back to join Bev at headquarters in Wheaton, Illinois. Now he was visiting his ailing mother in South Carolina. And he was not coming back.

How could this have happened? The Tindalls were successful missionaries. The perfect couple. They had met in church, introduced by Bev's college roommate. They had two dates before Gene left for active duty with the Air National Guard.

Eighty letters later, he returned and they got engaged. By Christmas, they were married.

Bible college and a successful pastorate followed. Gene threw himself into preaching, teaching, and visiting the sick. Bev had an active youth ministry and entertained frequently in their home. They were busy and, on the surface, happy.

But, says Bev, "Even though we had two little children, Gene's work always came first. It didn't seem to make any difference if I was sick or what."

The biggest issue for Bev, though, was her belief that Gene would love her more if she were thin. "I went on hundreds of diets. I was always trying to earn his love and of course that made me miserable. I would be jealous because he seemed to enjoy women who were younger and thinner."

Gene resented Bev's jealousy and constant need for reassurance. But instead of expressing his feelings, he retaliated the only way he knew how. "My weapon was a quasi-humorous sarcasm with a hook on it," says Gene. "It helped me avoid facing an issue head-on, but it left a bitter feeling."

If he had been able to talk with Bev about his feelings, they might have been able to deal with their problems early on. But having grown up in an emotionally closed family, Gene found it almost impossible to express himself.

After the pastorate, Bev and Gene went to Venezuela. Gene worked long hours, first as manager of the mission's bookstore and then as field director of the mission's work in eastern Venezuela. Bev worked part-time in the bookstore, carried on an active evangelistic ministry, and served as hostess to visiting missionaries. They were viewed as a model couple, but their relationship had become sterile.

"We were functioning as missionaries, we were praying together every night, we were even holding hands—but we weren't really communicating," says Gene. "A crust of emotions had built up that neither one of us was trying to break down."

Bev had tried to work through some issues early in their missionary experience. While they were still in language school she had said to Gene, "Honey, we've got to get some counseling. We're so incompatible." But Gene, by now highly experienced at putting a lid on his emotions, retorted, "We're not incompatible. We've got the best marriage there is."

So Bev assumed the problem was hers. "I had recurring depression," she recalls. "It was probably anger that I didn't want to deal with that turned into depression. A lot of it was my insecurity about Gene loving me. My parents divorced when I was six, after my father had been unfaithful to my mother, so I doubted men anyway. Then when Gene would show such obvious enjoyment of the young women who came down to work with us, I would be terribly jealous."

The tensions between them reached the point where it was a relief for them to get involved in their work—and get away from each other. Bev found satisfaction in soul-winning. Gene found someone else.

"We hired a secretary," he says, "a woman about twenty-two years old. I worked very closely with her and found myself attracted to her. She made me feel important and accepted. We began spending more and more time together. The attraction wasn't acknowledged at first, but later it became quite overt."

Bev was devastated, but Gene refused to admit what was going on—an emotional involvement that culminated in a brief infidelity. "I cried all the time," Bev says, "and was so depressed I hardly got dressed for about a month."

Finally, she and Gene called a family meeting with their two teenage children. "I told them, 'Dad and I are having some serious problems,'" recalls Bev. "'We just don't like each other anymore. My nerves are bad and I'm very sick. What shall we do?'"

The teenagers talked between themselves and finally suggested that Bev go back to the States to stay with her mother until she felt better. When their mission organization realized there were marital problems, Gene was asked to return home and they both were urged to seek counseling. Instead, Gene left for South Carolina and didn't come back.

They were apart for five years. Gene stayed in South Carolina, while Bev moved into missionary housing in Illinois. During this time, Gene and Bev saw each other only three times. Each time, they both had the same reaction: This is never going to work.

Convinced there was no chance he and Bev would get back together, Gene initiated divorce proceedings. "Then, right after I paid a lawyer to handle the case," he says, "I got a letter from the head of our mission." The mission executive offered to pay for Bev and Gene to spend two weeks at Marble Retreat, a Colorado-based program designed to help troubled Christian workers sort through their problems.

"I saw no hope," he says, "but I thought, 'Well, at least we'll settle this thing once and for all.' I figured the people at Marble Retreat would agree there was no way Bev and I could get back together."

Gene picked Bev up at the Denver airport to drive on to

Marble Retreat in western Colorado. The awkward silence in the car as they drove reminded her that they were strangers still.

Gene broke the silence long enough to worry out loud about sleeping arrangements: "Do these people realize we've been apart for five years? I'll stay on my side of the bed if you'll stay on yours." To the relief of both Gene and Bev, when they arrived at Marble Retreat their bedroom was equipped with twin beds.

"It was a lovely setting," recalls Bev. "We were in a rustic log cabin up in the mountains in the midst of beautiful scenery—without a single responsibility."

"We either had to talk or do nothing," adds Gene.

So talk they did. In daily group therapy sessions. During long afternoon walks. In their room at night. Day after day, they talked to each other—and to the hurting people around them. Some had marital problems; others were just burned out. For two weeks the routine was the same: Group therapy in the morning; time for walks or private sessions with Dr. Louis McBurney or his wife, Melissa, who directed the retreat, in the afternoon.

By the end of the first week, Gene began to feel remorse about what he had done to Bev. "I hadn't fully realized how much I had hurt her," he admits. "As she talked in the sessions, and we talked together in the afternoons, I came to understand that I had crushed her. And we both realized how much we had hurt our kids."

After listening to other couples talk, Gene began to think that maybe the problems he and Bev had weren't so insurmountable after all. But Bev, who had initially been hopeful, began to back away. The same characteristics about Gene that had bothered her in the past continued to bother her. Then she had a private talk with Melissa McBurney.

"Bev," Melissa said, "I get the feeling that you're just waiting for the two weeks to end so we can tell you, 'OK, you tried and it didn't work. Go ahead and get a divorce.' But we're not going to say that. If you would make up your mind to recommit to this marriage, we'd still have a few days to help you put it back together.

"You know," Melissa continued, "there are days I don't even like my husband. That's the way everybody is. That's why you have to look at your spouse as if you were focusing a camera—you just focus on what you want in the picture. The other things are still there, but you blur them out and focus on the positive things."

Listening to Louis McBurney, Gene came to a similar conclusion: "God made Bev the way she is and I'm not here to change her. I've got to accept her as she is. She's got her warts, but I've got mine, too."

In the end, says Gene, they recommitted themselves to each other "out of sheer will. There were no feelings of love. Just a sense that this is what God wants, no matter what happens."

So at the end of the two weeks, they decided to begin the process of merging their lives—again.

They began to work on issues that had been problems in the past, such as money management, the division of chores, and Gene's workaholism. "He decided to cut back on the hours he worked so we could spend more time together," explains Bev. "We began to go for walks, or bowl, or go out to dinner."

With more time together, Gene and Bev learned how to

communicate effectively. "When we'd go for walks or take long drives," says Gene, "we really began to talk. And we began to enjoy it."

As they became closer, they learned to understand how each expressed love: Bev mostly through doing things for Gene—ironing his shirts, making dinner; Gene mostly through words and physical affection. And they started working on ways to show love that the other would appreciate.

"When we first started working on this," says Gene, "it felt sort of artificial. But when we began to see the response, it really took on some meaning."

Forgiveness was another important component of the reconciliation process. Having forgiven each other for past actions and behavior, Bev and Gene learned to keep on forgiving. "When we have an argument now," explains Gene, "we get a good night's sleep and then the first thing we do is apologize. Because if you don't, you're going to build walls."

Both Gene and Bev feel strongly that getting outside help was critical in enabling them to get back together and learn to live with each other happily. The counseling they received at Marble Retreat and afterward helped them learn to talk to, listen to, and accept each other. It also gave them insight into how each of them had contributed to the near-demise of their marriage. Bev realized that her parents' divorce had left her with a lot of anger, insecurity, and distrust of men—all of which became focused on Gene. Gene realized that, as a child, he had learned to run and hide in the face of others' anger, a response he repeated when he ran from their marriage.

Ultimately, says Gene, the conviction that God wanted them to stay together was what saved their marriage. "Even when I filed for divorce," he explains, "I knew it was wrong. You've got to get to the point of being willing to sacrifice your own life to make your marriage work."

Bev remembers: "One day Melissa McBurney said, 'I get the impression that you think if you two get back together that God owes it to you to make you happy. But we're supposed to obey him whether or not it makes us happy.'" Ironically, it was when Gene and Bev finally gave up their right to happiness that they found it at last.

Perhaps the culmination of that happiness came the day their daughter got married. "I was so thrilled when Gene and I walked down the aisle together to light the candle," says Bev. "Just think of what we would have missed if we hadn't made the commitment to work things out."

Commentary

In many ways the story of Gene and Bev is a common one. The man starts out by being committed to and then becomes consumed by his work. Since he believes that real men work hard, the more he does the more successful he feels. As far as he is concerned the marriage is great. His wife tries to let him know there are problems but his denial is so strong her concerns and complaints may not even register with him. Or he writes it off to "she feels this way every month."

A wife will often ask her husband to go with her to talk with their pastor or a marriage counselor—but why should he, when everything is fine? Besides, if you are a

Christian leader you cannot let anyone know what you are going through because if they find out they might think less of you.

Over the years Bev and Gene drifted further and further apart and became married singles, strangers with a few things in common who lived under the same roof and shared the same last name.

There are very few things that are more important to a man's pride, his identity, his sense of value and worth, his manhood than work. That's why many men become addicted to their work; they become workaholics. There's a difference between loving what you do, having a passion for your work, and being a workaholic. If you can set your work down, let it go at the end of the day and not go through withdrawal, not ruminate about it throughout the evening or weekend, you aren't addicted to it.

Any addiction, even to work, serves to keep you separate from other people and from yourself and limits your ability to hear the voice of your heavenly Father. The problem isn't work: It is necessary and important. The problem is that many of us have allowed what we do to define our significance and to be the basis for our security. Work is inadequate on both counts. As you drift further and further from the Lord and from your spouse you become more vulnerable to sins that, at earlier points of your Christian life, you thought yourself incapable of. I'm sure that if, when he was pastoring his first church, you had asked Gene if he ever thought he would commit adultery he would have said no.

The story of Gene and Bev is a great illustration of the fact that it is never too late. They had been separated for five years and Gene had initiated divorce proceedings when they were asked to go to Marble Retreat in western Colorado. The decision they made opened the door to everything that followed. They decided to get help from professionals who were Christian, knew the Bible, understood people, and understood Christian leaders. They became willing to share their story with other hurting couples. A key piece of the healing process was Gene's willingness to take a look at his emotions from God's perspective.

A short time later Gene and Bev made another critical decision. It wasn't based on a warm moment or even feelings of love. They recommitted themselves to each other "out of sheer will." They chose to let go of their old relationship and work toward building a new relationship.

Over time and with much practice Gene and Bev learned how to communicate with each other. They began to understand and appreciate each other's uniqueness and learned how to communicate love in ways meaningful to their partner. They worked on forgiveness. Consistent with Psalm 139:23-24, they took responsibility for their own issues rather than constantly pointing out the other person's faults. Bev had gained an understanding of how her parents' divorce had negatively affected her ability to build a trusting relationship. Gene and Bev made time to get reacquainted. They walked, talked, and listened to each other and to wise counsel.

They shared with other couples. They gave up their "right" to happiness. They didn't wallow and stay stuck in a past they couldn't change. They chose to believe that their God was still in the business of making miracles.

The first letter of John is one of the most encouraging books in all of Scripture. In the first verse of chapter two he writes, "My dear children, I write this to you so that you will not sin." He is saying that God's will for us is that we don't sin. We are to do all that we can to avoid sin. If the text stopped there it would be rather discouraging. But it doesn't.

John immediately continues by saying, "But if anybody does sin, we have one who speaks to the Father in our defense—Jesus Christ, the Righteous One. He is the atoning sacrifice for our sins, and not only for ours but also for the sins of the whole world" (1 Jn 2:1-2). It's like God is saying through John, "Whatever you do, don't sin." But since he knows how we are made, since he understands the effects of sin on our life he adds, "But when you do sin I want you to remember where to look, who to turn to, and what to do."

It wasn't easy, it didn't happen overnight, and it didn't come without some pain. But today, because of hard work and God's help, Bev and Gene have a new marriage and a new hope.

Resources

Edward Bratcher, *The "Walk on Water" Syndrome* (Waco, Tex.: Word, 1984).

Les Carter, *Imperative People* (Nashville, Tenn.: Thomas Nelson, 1991).

Robert Hemfelt, Frank Minirth, and Paul Meier, *We Are Driven* (Nashville, Tenn.: Thomas Nelson, 1991).

Ed Wheat, *Love Life* (Grand Rapids, Mich.: Zondervan, 1980).

H. Norman Wright, *Communication: Key to Your Marriage* (Ventura, Calif.: Regal, 1980).

H. Norman Wright and Gary J. Oliver, *How to Bring Out the Best in Your Spouse* (Ann Arbor, Mich.: Servant, 1996).

Chapter 7

Eating Disorder
by Ron R. Lee

*W*hen Dan O'Neill met Cherry Boone, she was already well known in the entertainment world, having appeared in concerts and on television with her three sisters and their famous father, Pat Boone. But the fast-paced, show business lifestyle had taken a toll on Cherry's health. She struggled with anorexia nervosa, an obsession with weight loss. And by the time Dan met her, Cherry's disorder had moved into bulimia—a compulsive cycle of binge eating followed by self-induced vomiting and laxative abuse.

Dan felt confident that he could help Cherry overcome her self-destructive behavior. But neither of them was prepared for the pain, frustration, and humiliation they would suffer before Cherry would find a solution to her problem. The O'Neills have written Living on the Border of Disorder *(Bethany)* to show how family members can help a loved one recover from anorexia, bulimia, and other impulse-control disorders.

Cherry: My eating disorder was preceded by other problems, such as my low self-esteem and perfectionistic personality. I was always the "good girl." I didn't do things deliberately to upset my parents, and I tried to set a good example for my sisters. But I never felt that I measured up.

Things started to go downhill in the eighth grade when I took a class I wasn't doing well in. I avoided this class by pretending to be sick. While I was home, I would go on secret medicine-cabinet raids. That's when I found my mom's diet pills. When I took them, I could stay up all night and write A+ term papers for my other classes.

When the supply of pills ran low, I would order a refill in my mother's name, then I'd go pick it up myself. I missed forty days of school that year, and I got to drop the class I hated. I maintained my straight-A average, so my behavior was reinforced.

But I ended up digging a hole even deeper for myself. After one pill didn't make me feel as good as it used to, I started taking two. When the pills started disappearing faster, my mom suspected that I was taking them and canceled her prescription.

By then my sisters and I were doing a lot of performances. We were having pictures taken and going for costume fittings. It was important that I maintain my weight. But without diet pills, I went from 113 pounds to 140, and my problem became a weight-control issue. I felt the pressure to look perfect, so I started a severe diet and exercise routine. I dropped to 116 pounds, and I received praise from everyone, which encouraged me to continue.

By the time I was sixteen, I was jogging four miles every day before school. I would usually skip breakfast and lunch. After school, I'd ride my bike, do two hours of calisthenics, and swim. Then I'd eat a normal dinner.

When my weight dropped to 92 pounds, my parents pressured me to eat more. When I did, I found my body demanded more and more nutrition. I began bingeing, but I was so fearful of getting fat that I counteracted my eating binges by forcing myself to vomit and by taking laxatives. I realized this was abnormal, but I didn't seem to have any control over it.

Cherry's eating disorder was growing more and more dangerous, damaging her health and changing her character. A teenager who had grown up in a strict Christian family, she found herself resorting to deception to conceal her bingeing and purging. She shoplifted high-calorie snack foods, as well as laxatives, to feed her compulsion without being detected by her parents. By age twenty, when Cherry met Dan O'Neill, her deception was well practiced.

Cherry: When my relationship with Dan started getting serious, I told him about my eating disorder. He didn't seem overly concerned about it. As I came to realize later, Dan was a driven, "can-do" type of guy. He was confident that he could help me overcome my problem.

One night after Dan had taken me out to dinner, he was afraid I would be tempted to binge and purge at home. So he made me promise I wouldn't eat anything else that night. After he dropped me off, he walked back to the car and I went into the kitchen. I noticed some leftover lamb chops in the dog's dish, and I impulsively squatted on the floor and started eating the scraps.

For some reason, Dan came back to the door. He knocked

on the window and there I was, eating out of the dog's dish. Both of us were horrified.

Dan: Because of incidents such as that, Cherry knew I didn't trust her in the area of her eating disorder. After we got married in 1975, I wondered if trust would be a problem in *other* areas. But I could see that she didn't spend money irresponsibly, and I knew she was faithful to me. Plus, by that time, Cherry seemed to have her bingeing and purging under control.

Cherry: But I didn't have it under control. We had been married several weeks when I decided to tell Dan I was still struggling with bulimia. When I told him, he felt I had been dishonest because I had waited so long to let him know. So instead of giving me the supportive reaction he had given before we were married, *this* time he started withdrawing from me. His negative response solidified my tendency to be deceptive because I felt that if I were honest with him I would be rejected.

This incident was an early indication that our marriage would become intertwined with the destructive effects of my eating disorder. In hindsight, we can see that my bulimia affected our marriage as much as it posed a threat to my health.

Dan: At that time I didn't know that Cherry's deception was part and parcel of anorexia, bulimia, and other impulse-control disorders. Back then, things were more black and white in my thinking. To me, she was simply being dishonest.

In time, Dan returned to his long-established pattern of trying to fix every big problem he encountered. In the past, he had always succeeded. But Cherry's problem was different.

"I was trying to figure out how I could make Cherry stop eating too much and stop purging," he says. "It became a control issue." But when attempts at controlling her behavior failed, Dan tried to force Cherry to face her problem head-on.

Dan: As soon as I'd leave for work, Cherry would prepare a calorie-packed chocolate drink. She would drink it and then vomit. One morning I returned home unexpectedly and interrupted her in the middle of her secret binge. After that, I wondered every day what she might be doing behind my back.

I thought if I could confront her with evidence of her bingeing and purging, it would force her to face her problem. So I decided to hunt for food wrappers in the dumpster at our apartment complex. I found a bag full of trash with an empty brown-sugar box on top. I had seen a similar box in our kitchen that day. Inside the bag were candy wrappers, ice-cream cartons, cookie bags, doughnut boxes, and an empty laxative box. I confronted Cherry with all this evidence, but she lied and said it was someone else's.

Cherry: I would deny what I was doing even in the face of clear evidence to the contrary. It got to the point where Dan would mark the lids on food containers, and then check to see if I had opened them. He also marked the level of the food in other containers and checked them later to see if the level had gone down.

With my own husband acting like the CIA, I felt I had to

get sneakier, so I'd shoplift laxatives and take them before I went home. I didn't want to do these things, yet I wasn't able to control it.

Cherry's health was declining week by week, and the O'Neills were both praying for help. But they say they never did ask God to instantly bail them out of their problems.

Dan: I didn't pray for a big miracle because I believe God has given us enough free choice to kill ourselves, if that's what we choose to do. And actually, that's what Cherry was doing by gradually starving herself. At that point I didn't pray for anything other than God's provision for our day-to-day, moment-by-moment needs. We were trying to find the interior graces that God provides to help us get through this. Our spiritual pilgrimage and the healing pilgrimage were linked in many ways.

Cherry: We didn't know how this was all going to end, but we realized that God wanted it to work out for our good. The fact that we knew he was with us kept us going.

Dan: But we still had to find a way out of this problem. Less than two years into our marriage, Cherry's weight dropped to eighty pounds and she agreed to enter a hospital. Her doctor pulled me aside and said, "I want to talk to you straight. Cherry needs a psychiatric profile." On another occasion, he told me: "You need to get out of Los Angeles."

My work stress, Cherry's show business career, and the demands being made on us by family members and others were making it difficult for Cherry and me to focus on our marriage and on overcoming her eating disorder. The doctor was right—we needed to take drastic action.

Cherry: Leaving LA would have far-reaching effects. I had entered into contracts to perform with my sisters and my dad. Our doctor said, "There are no contracts when it comes to life and death." But I still felt like such a failure—I was letting everybody down. I had to cancel contracts after the costumes, the choreography, and all the vocal arrangements had already been done and paid for.

Dan: While Cherry remained in the hospital, I boxed things up at home. I had an uncle who was pastor of a church in Seattle, and my parents lived near him. They said we could live with them until we got settled.

Cherry: Dan's uncle had gone through a depression caused by heart medication. Dr. Raymond Vath, a psychotherapist who attended his church, helped him work his way out of that severe depression. We thought Dr. Vath might be able to help us.

Dan: We said good bye to secure employment at the same time we were saying hello to tens of thousands of dollars in medical bills. We had to abandon ourselves to Divine Providence. But it was the right move.

Cherry: In therapy, I learned that because I had been a perfectionist, I had no self-esteem left. I needed to find something about myself that was worthwhile that wasn't based on what I did, or how well I did it, or what I looked like.

Dr. Vath also helped me see that I was slowly committing suicide, that subconsciously I wanted to die. And he helped Dan work on his tendency to try to control me. Once Dan started to take the heavy control off of me, it put me in a position of having to take responsibility for myself.

Cherry started dealing with the issues that lay behind her eating disorder. She says anyone struggling with anorexia or bulimia needs to deal with certain "foundational issues" before she can recover.

Cherry: I had to deal with my perfectionism and low self-esteem, as well as the inappropriate guilt that weighed me down. I still struggle somewhat with perfectionism, but we all need to realize that doing your best is good enough. It's OK to have limitations, and it's OK to make mistakes.

Dan: Once Cherry got control of her eating disorder, we had to deal with our pattern of relating to each other on the basis of Cherry being sick and me trying to help her get well. The healing process required a complete reorientation in our relationship.

Cherry: I knew I was trustworthy, but Dan was still suspicious of me in certain areas because that was how he was used to relating to me. It took awhile for me to realize, "I know I'm OK, and that's going to have to be enough until he gets to the point where *he* knows I'm OK." That is where I started to build up my own self-confidence and identity.

Dan: I could see Cherry was making good decisions and that she was building a track record of recovery. But we had to work through a lot of hurt, alienation, confusion, and anger. It took time for all that to dissipate.

Cherry: And we still had to deal with the physiological consequences of my eating disorder. My reproductive system had shut down. My uterus had atrophied, and I wasn't having a menstrual cycle. Both of us, independently of one another, prayed about that situation. Within a few months my reproductive system kicked in, and three months later I was pregnant. To me that was God's stamp of approval on the healing process. I felt he was saying, "Now you're not only able to deal with your own life, but I'm willing to trust you with another one." We now have five children, four daughters and one son. After all we've been through together, Dan said to me one time: "Maybe there would have been somebody better as a husband for you than me." I told him, "There's no doubt in my mind that we were absolutely right for each other. If I hadn't met you, I wouldn't have worked so hard to recover from this disorder. If it hadn't been for you, I wouldn't have learned how to be strong on my own. And if it weren't for me, you would have never come to terms with your own humanity by facing an obstacle that you couldn't conquer."

Dan: As a result of this ordeal, Cherry learned that she can't be dependent on the praise and approval of others. We also learned the meaning of the wedding vows we took—our commitment was severely tested, "in sickness and in health." More than ever, we experienced the grace, mercy, and faithfulness of God.

Update: Today Cherry and Dan are helping the hungry through Mercy Corps International (www.mercycorps.org).

Commentary

Eating disorders. Everyone's heard about them but there are still many who don't understand what they really are, how to recognize them, or the devastation they can bring. Eating disorders fall into two major categories: anorexia nervosa and bulimia. They have been around for a long time but have never affected more people than they do today.

In some ways anorexia is the most dangerous cycle of eating disorders. Approximately 7 percent of its sufferers will die from drastic, painful, self-imposed caloric restrictions. Most anorexics are eighteen to twenty-five years old, but the disorder can also strike later in life. Approximately 95 percent are women. Anorexia starts with restricting the intake of food as part of a drive for thinness. It seems innocent enough. Over time the person becomes obsessed with losing weight and claims to "feel fat" even when those around her contradict her observation.

Over time the anorexic can develop bizarre eating habits, such as cutting food in tiny pieces and chewing each piece a certain number of times, compulsive exercising, progressive social isolation, an increased obsession with overachieving, and a desire for perfection. The numerous psychological features include denial, avoidance of conflict, a pervasive sense of helplessness, low self-esteem to the point of being depressed, and an inability to make choices. It's important to note that most anorexics don't see their behavior as abnormal.

It's easy for anorexia to lead to bulimia, which has reached epidemic proportions. It can be more difficult to identify someone who is struggling with bulimia because, unlike anorexics, bulimics are often close to their normal weight. However, they maintain their weight through dangerous binges and purges.

A binge involves the person consuming large amounts of food in a short time and then eliminating it by vomiting, abusing laxatives and diuretics, fasting, or engaging in excessive exercise. Once established, the behavior is hard to stop.

The medical complications of bulimia are numerous and include ulcers, dizziness, fainting, swollen salivary glands, eroded teeth (from the stomach acid brought up during vomiting), a chronically sore throat, rupture of the stomach or esophagus, and chronic sinusitis from residual vomitus in the sinus cavities.

Here are seven signs of bulimia to look for in yourself or a loved one:

1. You don't care what it is you eat—you just have to eat something.
2. You eat food very fast. Most binges are over in two hours.
3. You can't stop at a single portion—you must have the whole bag or box.
4. If you run out of the food you're craving, you'll go to great lengths to get more.
5. You feel you must hide while you're bingeing—and you'll try to hide the "evidence."

6. You feel tremendous guilt and self-reproach when you finish.
7. You plan to make up for today's overeating tomorrow.

The story of Cherry and Dan is not weird or unusual. The progression of Cherry's sickness is typical of how it happens.

The O'Neills started the healing process by acknowledging that there was a problem, reaching out for help, and becoming willing to do whatever is necessary to get well. Dan decided to do even something as drastic as moving to save his wife. Sometimes it takes a medical crisis and involuntary hospitalization for the person to get a wake-up call and begin to turn around, but it doesn't have to come to that. Given the potentially fatal nature of an eating disorder one of the first steps needs to be an appointment for a complete physical with a physician who understands eating disorders.

In addition to ongoing medical treatment there is a need for professional Christian counseling to learn about oneself, the disorder, and the healing process. Once again, the therapist needs to understand eating disorders. The numerous psychological, emotional, and relational aspects must be dealt with from a biblical perspective. The person's tendency toward perfectionism and the accompanying feelings of inadequacy, unworthiness, and guilt need to be addressed. Remember, the core issue in eating disorders isn't food or weight. It is the unrealistically high expectations of achievement the person places on herself.

It's easier for some to focus on their bodies and their flaws than to deal with the real issues in their lives.

Along the way the O'Neills made good decisions. They availed themselves of spiritual resources and did not give up on God or on each other. They took the initiative to see a physician and receive wise counsel. They heeded the advice they were given. Each one began to take responsibility for his or her own issues that affected the dynamics of their relationship. They acknowledged God's goodness and mercy to them.

Perhaps you have noticed similar patterns in someone and wonder if she could be struggling with the early stages of an eating disorder. Here are seven symptoms; if you or someone you know has even three of these I encourage you to talk to a Christian counselor who is familiar with eating disorders.

1. Sudden or severe weight gain or loss.
2. Frequent fluctuation of weight.
3. Food hoarding.
4. Amenorrhea (cessation of menstruation).
5. Skipping meals and eating alone.
6. Frequent nausea, bloating, or constipation.
7. Exaggerated fear of gaining weight.

At the end of their book Dan writes, "I must say that if this book is built on any one theme, it is hope. In our darkest years it was the mere flickering memory of hope that allowed hope itself to resurface as a point of light at the end of a dark tunnel. It was hope based on faith that provided the emotional energy for the long journey to health."

Resources

Cherry Boone O'Neill, *Starving for Attention* (New York: Continuum, 1982).

Dan and Cherry O'Neill, *Living on the Border of Disorder* (Minneapolis: Bethany, 1992).

Remuda Ranch: Center for Anorexia and Bulimia, One East Apache Street, Wickenburg, Ariz. 85390. 520-684-3913.

Cynthia Joye Rowland, *The Monster Within: Overcoming Bulimia* (Grand Rapids, Mich.: Baker, 1984).

Pam Vredevelt and Joyce Whitman, *Walking a Thin Line* (Portland, Ore.: Multnomah, 1985).

"Wasting Away: Eating Disorders on Campus," *People*, April 12, 1999: 53–72.

Marlene Boskind-White and William C. White, Jr., *Bulimarexia: The Binge/Purge Cycle* (New York: Norton, 1983).

Chapter 8

Keeping Secrets
by Gregg Lewis

E arly in 1972 Specialist Fifth-Class Randy Robertson returned to the United States from a nine-month tour of duty in Vietnam as a medic with the 82nd Airborne Division. His plane landed in San Diego.

"The war was winding down at that point," he remembers. "We were bringing home two men for every one we were sending over.

"I'd known I was about to be drafted soon after I graduated from college, so I enlisted and applied for the medical corps. As an enlistee, I figured to get assigned to Germany; at least that was the plan."

Draftees got sent to Vietnam. And during the war the biggest percentage of draftees were poor and poorly educated—those who had dropped out of school, or flunked out. Which meant most of Randy's college friends, like a lot of Americans who opposed the war, considered those who fought in Vietnam not only morally wrong but dumb for ending up there in the first place.

"I didn't want to be seen as dumb or wrong," Randy says. "So I certainly didn't want to go to Vietnam. But the Army had a shortage of combat medics, so despite the fact I'd enlisted and been promised duty in Europe, Vietnam was where they sent me.

"I'd seen a lot of protests before I went, but even though I'd anticipated some disapproval after I got back home, I wasn't prepared for what happened in the San Diego airport. There were five of us in uniform who walked off the plane together. And just as we entered through the gate door into the terminal we were greeted by a group of protesters who bombarded us with dead roses and called us 'baby-killers.'

"That was my first impression of my country's attitude toward my participation in the Vietnam War." That first impression stuck. The happiness Randy felt at being back in the States was overshadowed by the shame and disapproval he felt for having gone.

Some people might have shrugged off the harsh public opinion, but Randy seemed particularly vulnerable. He had worked to earn the approval of others all his life. From the time he was a young child he had felt he could never measure up to his brothers' academic accomplishments. No matter what he achieved or how hard he tried, he didn't think he could ever satisfy his parents. He found success in athletics, but his parents didn't value athletics. All three of his brothers went to exclusive private colleges; Randy went to a state school on a baseball scholarship. So as he says, "I felt like just another dumb jock." And then, of course, like a lot of athletes, Randy had to contend with the harsh judgment of demanding coaches.

"I remember my junior year in college I fought to get my

batting average over .400 for the season. I finished with a mark of .420-something, leading the Southeastern Conference and fifth in the country in major college baseball. But at the end of the season when my coach came up to me and said, 'You know you should have hit .500,' I suddenly felt as if I'd accomplished nothing. No matter what I did, I could never seem to measure up."

Randy's lifelong longing—to win the approval of others—helps explain the deep sense of rejection he felt upon arriving home from Vietnam. "I might have walked into an airport men's room and changed into civilian clothes," he says, "but I didn't have any."

What he did was strip his uniform of all medals and ribbons that indicated he had been in Vietnam (including two Purple Hearts and a Silver Star awarded for valor in battle). "I actually threw the medals away," Randy says. "I didn't want anything on my uniform that would identify me with the war."

Within a couple of weeks, he found a way to ditch the entire uniform. He signed up for a hitch in the National Guard, turned in his regular army uniform and donned the more "respectable" uniform of a Guardsman. "All my service records were transferred to the Guard, and when anyone asked if I'd been in Vietnam, I'd just say, 'I joined the National Guard.'" The truth served as a lie.

In addition to camouflaging his war record, duty in the National Guard served a second purpose. "I knew it would improve my chances of getting a job. The image so many people had of Vietnam veterans was that we were either violent, emotionally disturbed, or drug addicts. Men who had operated million-dollar equipment one week in Vietnam would be home the next week and not be trusted to drive a cab." By being able to tell prospective employers he was a Guardsman, Randy hoped to avoid the stigma of an "unstable Vietnam vet."

An All-American baseball player at the University of Alabama, Randy had played minor league ball in the St. Louis Cardinals organization for a season before enlisting in the Army. His sports background, his medic training in the military, and his "respectable" position in the National Guard helped him land a position as an assistant director at a Christian camp in rural Alabama. Living and working for two years away from civilization in the peaceful outdoors made it easier to leave behind the memories of a war he wanted to forget.

"If I acted as if I had never gone to Vietnam, then I wouldn't have to deal with those guilty feelings that I hadn't done enough to try to save the men I had to leave behind."

It was while he was working at that rural Alabama camp that Randy decided to leave the camp to work for Youth for Christ, a national evangelism organization. It was during the internship training for his new position that he met and began dating Meg Robinson, another intern.

When Meg, who thought Randy was a sharp, capable guy, realized he didn't have any confidence in his own abilities, she deliberately set out to show him she believed in him. That made Meg different from anyone else Randy had ever known.

Their friendship developed. When the subject of his military service eventually came up, he automatically told Meg what he told everyone else: He was in the National Guard. But because people falling in love invariably want to know and understand more about each other's backgrounds, Randy's "truthful" lie wasn't enough.

Meg told him she had known guys who had gone to Vietnam and come home as emotional wrecks. He didn't want her to be wary of him, so he didn't risk admitting he'd been there. Instead, he explained that he had enlisted in the Army just before being drafted, had gone to jump school at Ft. Bragg in preparation for being assigned to Vietnam, and at the last minute had been given the option of joining the National Guard. Again a lot of truth mixed with the one big lie.

As his relationship with Meg grew more serious, Randy thought from time to time that he ought to tell her the truth. "I told myself I'd tell her someday. But I hoped it would never have to come out."

A year after they met, Randy and Meg got married and did Christian youth work in Georgia before moving to Dallas, where Randy took a position on a church staff as the youth minister.

"I had a time of culture shock after moving from California to the deep South," Meg says. "But those were exciting years early in our marriage. We enjoyed working together. We'd do lots of spur-of-the-moment fun things. Marriage was more of a fun adjustment than a difficult adjustment."

"And yet, little things would crop up," Randy recalls. "One time when we were talking about buying a house, Meg said, 'Wouldn't it be great to be able to get a Veterans Administration loan?' I had to tell her, 'But we can't, because I was just in the Guard.' Of course, that was a direct lie."

Years passed. The lies multiplied. "Here I was preaching to kids, teaching them about the Bible and Christianity, living as a Christian with a Christian wife and a Christian marriage, and I was a big liar."

Sometimes he felt terribly guilty. Other times he found it easy to justify the deception. "I told myself it was OK for me to lie in this case because other people wouldn't understand the truth. And I would look at other people, other Christians even, and think what I was doing wasn't bad at all compared to what they were doing."

The longer he kept the secret, the bigger the stakes. Randy had always told himself he'd tell Meg the truth "someday." But somewhere along the line he passed what felt like the point of no return. And now he told himself there'd be more harm done in telling the truth than in continuing the lie. To tell the truth now could hurt his ministry and his marriage. That thinking bought him even more time.

By this stage Randy had suppressed the truth for so long that a lot of the memories he wanted to forget were buried deep in his subconscious. Yet from time to time something would trigger the memories and remind him of the truth he was hiding.

"For a couple of years there seemed to be stories every week in the newspaper about one more crazed Vietnam veteran who'd cracked under pressure and killed his family, shot his boss, or was barricaded in some building, threatening to blow himself and his hostages up. And while those news reports reminded me that I had some things of my own to work out about Vietnam, they made me all the more afraid to tell the truth. I certainly didn't want to be seen as one more disturbed Vietnam vet. So the suppression and denial continued. But it was becoming like a cancer eating away at my insides."

The dissonance in his life finally got to Randy. He went to a counselor at the church, a professional he knew had counseled other Vietnam vets. "I went intending to tell her," he says. "But I spent most of the session beating around the bush asking about people she had counseled and about other things. Finally, I said, 'You've talked to a lot of Vietnam veterans, right?'

"She nodded. 'Yes.'

"I guess it dawned on her, because she asked, 'Did you go to Vietnam, Randy?'

"'Well, uh, you don't think all Vietnam veterans are bad, do you?' I asked. Virginia looked at me and said, 'You didn't answer my question. Did you go to Vietnam?'

"'I kinda did,' I said.

"'How long were you kinda there?' she asked. 'What was your "kinda experience" like?'

"So I started kinda telling her."

For the next few months Randy went regularly for counseling. He talked about the shame he felt, the lack of acceptance he had feared if people knew he'd gone to Vietnam. And he talked about the horrors of war he had witnessed and had tried to block out.

"I remember, not long after I got to 'Nam, sitting in the back of a truck with other GIs when a little Vietnamese boy, only about five or six years old, came walking toward us. Our sergeant jumped up and shot the boy with his M-16 and I started yelling in shock, 'What are you doing?'

"But when I went to examine that little body with four bullet holes in the chest I saw what that sergeant had seen. The Viet Cong had strapped explosives to that boy and sent him to us. If the sergeant hadn't shot him, he'd have been blown up and maybe killed all of us as well.

"Did American soldiers kill women and children in Vietnam? Yes. But what people have to understand is that a lot of women and children had AK-47s and were shooting at us. When someone starts shooting at you, trying to kill you, you shoot back.

"In every war civilians are caught in the middle. Thousands of women and children were killed when we bombed Germany during World War II. Thousands more were killed at Hiroshima and Nagasaki. War is never humane."

In Vietnam, even humane acts often triggered more atrocity. Randy recalls one such event: "One day we went out into the bush to vaccinate a village's children. As a medic I gave the actual vaccinations. The next day we went back and discovered the Viet Cong had retaliated against the village's cooperation with us by hacking off the arms of every child who had been vaccinated. I'll never forget the sickening horror of seeing the pile of human arms outside that village."

After six months, Randy's counselor told him she thought it was time he confess his lies and tell Meg about his Vietnam experience. "I'd jumped out of airplanes and been shot at in rice paddies and that was nothing compared to the courage I needed to tell Meg the truth," he says. "I prayed and prayed, asking God to help me. But I was still scared."

Finally he did it. After almost eight years of marriage Randy faced Meg and told her the truth. Their memories of the details differ somewhat, but they agree that that night was a turning point.

Randy remembers: "I walked into the room and said, 'Meg, I feel I ought to share something with you.' I swallowed hard and said right out, 'I'm sorry I've been lying to you. I was in Vietnam.'

"Meg laughed and said, 'Come on, Randy. What do you want to tell me?'

"I said, 'I'm not teasing. I served in Vietnam.' She didn't believe me."

Meg remembers Randy starting to talk about Vietnam. At first she was confused because she couldn't figure out whose experience he was talking about. "When Randy said he'd gone to Vietnam, I thought he was joking. He kept insisting and I remember him getting angry because I wasn't believing him."

Randy says, "I told her I was sorry I'd lied about the National Guard. 'Then where did you go on those weekends?' she wanted to know. I told her I had been in the Guard and explained why."

"I eventually realized he was serious," Meg recalls. "But it still didn't make any sense to me. I started quizzing him in an attempt to trip him up. That upset him more because I still wasn't believing the story. However, the more he told me, the more I realized the pieces did fit in the cracks between the details I had known about Randy. It seemed possible that what he was saying was true.

"That made me angry. I said to myself, 'If Randy loved me, why would he lie to me all these years?' By the time Randy quit answering my questions that night I think I'd describe my feelings as half anger, half disbelief. And those feelings lasted for a long time.

"I'd known guys who had come back from Vietnam who were plagued by flashbacks and addicted to drugs. For years I'd been grateful to God that Randy had avoided the trauma of that war. Now here he was telling me he'd been through it after all."

Telling Meg the truth relieved some of the pressure that had been building up inside Randy for years. But he admits, "I was angry that Meg was angry. I had told the truth, and I felt that we should now put it behind us. But I needed to understand that my confession wasn't the end of the problem. I'd finally told the truth, but it would take time for the resentment to work out. It would take time to rebuild trust."

According to Meg, "It was months before I quit asking entrapment-type questions about his experience in Vietnam, trying to make sure he was telling me the truth. And I began reading about Vietnam vets who had blacked out their entire war experience and denied the whole thing. That I could understand because I'd blacked out almost a year of my life as a child when my parents went through a terrible divorce.

"I had a much harder time understanding why he felt ashamed of his time in Vietnam when he'd saved so many lives. What saddens me most today is that Randy was awarded a Silver Star and two Purple Hearts for some very brave acts. I wish we had those medals for our boys to see and for Randy to have to remind himself of how brave he was, how he went back time and again to rescue guys dying in rice paddies.

"But after he told me he'd been to Vietnam, it took me a couple of years to work through the anger and believe he really loved me. I'd think, 'If he lied about that, what else has he lied about?' It took time for me to get to the point where I knew I could trust him, that what he said was truth. And it also took two years for me to mature to the point of realizing my role in accepting Randy, showing him how proud I was of him and by doing that, helping him to heal. I need to say that it was Jesus Christ who helped me work it through."

Looking back Randy says, "I wish now I'd done it earlier so we could have worked through those issues much sooner in our marriage. It was hard, but our marriage is stronger now. And we can communicate at a much deeper and more honest level. Without God's help we really couldn't have done it."

Commentary

In some ways Randy was set up for his reaction by events that took place long before the war. A person who grows up in a home where he's told that nothing he or she does is ever good enough often responds by doing whatever is necessary to get some kind of praise, applause, and approval. It's easy for that person to become a people pleaser who can be driven by fear of rejection.

Not only was Randy blindsided by a mountain of repressed fear he hadn't anticipated, he was also forced to do hand-to-hand combat with his guilt. He had received basic training to be a soldier. He hadn't received any training for this emotional battle. From his perspective the only way he could deal with it was to ignore it. Randy discovered that guilt, like other emotions, can be either healthy or unhealthy. Healthy guilt usually comes from two sources. The first is civil or legal guilt, which involves a violation of society's law. The second is spiritual guilt, which involves a violation of God's clearly revealed law.

Unhealthy or destructive guilt is an emotional experience that may not relate to anything we have done. That was the case with Randy's guilt. He had done the best he could in an unbelievably difficult situation. But the tyranny of second-guessing combined with the "shoulds" and "oughts" and "what-ifs" led him down a path of unhealthy guilt and unnecessary self-condemnation.

Randy says the fear and guilt-driven deception became "like a cancer eating away at my insides." One of his first important decisions was to say that enough was enough. He found the courage to reach out for help to someone who could listen, understand, and help him make sense of the myriad of confusing emotions. He also reached out to God. Sometimes the first step in breaking through our fear involves admitting our fear by simply saying to ourselves, to God, and perhaps to others, "I am afraid." There can be tremendous freedom in having the strength and courage to take the first step and admit that we are experiencing fear.

After six months of counseling Randy was convinced that he needed to tell Meg the truth. For someone who had survived Vietnam, seen what he had seen, won several medals, you'd think it wouldn't be that big a deal. But it was. Telling the truth to himself and then to Meg was the essential first step, but it didn't magically solve the problem. Now Randy was faced with dealing with the consequences of his deception and lies—disbelief, hurt feelings, anger, and broken trust. The rebuilding and healing process would take some time.

While healing always takes time—in this case a few years—there are several important things that Meg and Randy did to accelerate the process of recovery and restoration. After the admission of the lie they worked to build a new relationship on honesty and truth. They tried to have some fun, they worked at building their friendship with each other, they shared their hopes and dreams, they became involved in ministry together.

Meg had the maturity to realize that Randy wasn't the only one God wanted to work on. There were some issues in her own life that God wanted to address. They went for Christian counseling and dealt with many emotions, including the difficult emotion of anger. Meg was angry at Randy and Randy was angry at Meg's anger. Meg might have wondered how, if Randy really loved her, he could have lied to her. Randy might have wondered how, if Meg really loved him, she could be mad at him for having the courage to risk the rejection that might come from telling the truth.

How they chose to respond to the anger was another important decision in the trust-building process. In a previous chapter we saw that anger is always secondary to hurt, frustration, or fear. With God's help and some wise counsel they chose to move through the past hurt, the present frustration, and the future fear to trust God's love for them and their love for each other.

You may never have been to Vietnam and you may never have lied to your spouse as Randy did. But you may be struggling with guilt and fear from a different source. You too can discover what Randy and Meg discovered, that God helps us overcome all our fears.

Resources

William Backus and Marie Chapian, *Telling Yourself the Truth* (Minneapolis: Bethany, 1980).

William Backus, *Telling Each Other the Truth* (Minneapolis: Bethany, 1991).

Susan Forward, *When Your Lover Is a Liar* (New York: Harper-Collins, 1999).

Gary J. Oliver, *Real Men Have Feelings Too* (Chicago: Moody Press, 1993).

John Powell, *Why Am I Afraid to Tell You Who I Am?* (Allen, Tex.: Resources for Christian Living, 1995).

H. Norman Wright, *The Healing of Fears* (Eugene, Ore.: Harvest House, 1982).

——, *Winning Over Your Emotions* (Eugene, Ore.: Harvest House, 1998).

Chapter 9

Premarital Sex
by Rodney Clapp

O f all the marriages I know well, here are some vital facts
about the one I admire the most:

- Elise and Martin "had" to get married.
- She was twenty and pregnant; he was nineteen.
- Her parents were divorced when she was thirteen; his parents are still together but fought horribly when he was a boy, and three of his father's five brothers have been divorced.
- Their baby lived one day after she was born.

For a marriage to survive after such a rocky beginning would
be surprise enough. But this one has done more than survive:
Elise and Martin clearly and deeply prize their life together.
How has this come to be?

Martin and Elise met at college, a Christian school on the
East Coast. Elise remembers an English literature class during
the first semester: "I saw Martin walk in with his curly hair,

pink shirt, and white painter's pants. I thought, 'He's really good looking, and I'm going to get to know him.'"

She went to college for an education, but "wanted to find a husband and was scoping guys out from the beginning."

They studied together for a few weeks before their first date. The date, like many to come, was a movie. There was plenty of fun. In many ways they were good for each other. Martin had enjoyed other relationships, but the affirmation had never been mutual—he loved her, but she did not love him, or vice versa. "With Elise I had the first relationship that felt like a really strong bond and I went after that like crazy." Elise was attracted by a male who was gentle and quiet; her father was aggressive and loud.

But there were some clouds in their relationship. Looking back, Martin says, "We were two very, very needy people." Elise says, "Our neuroses meshed. I was over-responsible, Martin was under-responsible." She offers an example. "In our lit class, we had to interpret poems. I was assigned 'Hap,' by Thomas Hardy, which is only three stanzas long. Martin was assigned 'The Rime of the Ancient Mariner,' which is about fifty pages. We got permission to trade poems." Martin shakes his head: "And then she did 'Hap,' too."

Another ambiguous element was sex. Elise believes "the glue holding us together was our physical attraction." As Martin understands it, "My neediness was expressed and satisfied in sexual terms." Their involvement escalated when Elise went home with Martin at Christmas, but it was confined to petting, until the following spring break.

At spring break Martin visited Elise at her home. Her bedroom was across the hall from that of her stepfather and mother. Late one evening, Martin came in to say good night. Things got out of hand. In what followed the two of them were as together as two people can be physically, but in another sense they were radically apart.

Says Martin, "We had been as close as you can get without having sex. At the time I thought it was exciting, that we were inching toward this new plateau. I had no idea Elise felt the way she did."

Says Elise, "I didn't want to have sex but I had this feeling of powerlessness. I had a history of viewing my body as something to be given in exchange for love and affection. Part of the tragedy of the situation had to do with hoping this was a true Christian relationship and that it was going to last a lifetime. Even as we made love, I had a tremendous sense of disappointment in myself."

Here is the way it was for her: "We were petting and then at a certain point I clicked into a mode of 'OK, this is what is going to happen. This is it. I'm just here.' It was horrible."

Immediately afterward Elise began weeping uncontrollably. She could hardly talk enough to explain her feelings. At one point she left her room and went into Martin's, curling up on the bed. He knelt beside her and wrapped his arms around her. Martin was puzzled, guilty, and sad. "She was crying and crying. It wasn't very difficult to be sympathetic to this person who was"—he searches for the word—"shattered."

Martin and Elise contended with sexual temptation through the remainder of the school year. Elise was beginning to have doubts about the future of the relationship, and these were cemented when they departed to their separate homes for the summer. Her church, a significant factor in her life, emphasized celibacy until marriage, as well as the importance of the God-relationship above all others. She broke up with Martin over the telephone and returned his high school ring through the mail.

It was not a bad summer for Elise. She was surrounded and supported by her church friends. But Martin sank into depression: "I felt like the only person who had ever loved me was gone."

They both returned to school with trepidation. The first day back, there was a barbecue on campus. As Martin recalls, "Elise stood there with a girlfriend, trying to look the other way. My heart was exploding in my chest." Elise assured him she wanted to be friends; Martin wondered how, now that they had made love together.

The pair spent "enormous amounts" of time together that fall. It was, in Elise's estimation, "a nice time." Sex was out of the picture. They took walks, practicing their rudimentary French in conversation. They went out with friends. But beneath the careful rhetoric, Martin thought he sensed deep feelings for him in Elise. He determined to win her back.

Late in the fall they walked in a local park. The leaves were turning; it was cold and gray. They ended up holding hands. Martin told Elise he wanted to get back together. The relationship wasn't clearly defined, but she agreed to be his date at Winterfest, an elaborate campus event to come in February.

Winterfest peaked with a formal banquet, tuxedos and gowns expected. Martin and Elise attended proudly, happily. By this time they were a couple again. After the banquet they went out for dessert with friends. Back on campus they found an isolated spot and made out more heavily than they had since their courtship resumed.

The next night they went to a movie, one Elise says she still hates. It was the sexually charged *An Officer and a Gentleman.* Elise thinks that maybe they were "revved up" from the night before. Anyway, after the movie they found a spot beneath a stairwell in the basement of her dormitory. "It's the only time we had sex that year, so we know that's when I got pregnant."

A few weeks later came spring break. At home Elise talked to her mother and a girlfriend; they accompanied her to a pregnancy testing center run by a pro-life organization. She remembers being called into a back room with her mother. The test was positive. "There was a roaring in my ears. I was totally blitzed."

At home she telephoned Martin, who was in Florida visiting a friend. Then she settled down to wait in a furious welter of emotions. She was deeply ashamed. "It's weird, but I withdrew and became a totally different person. I had been gregarious, extroverted, always the center of attention, a leader. It all changed. I lost confidence. It was like the dark side of me."

She felt terribly vulnerable. She trusted Martin's honor, but she was afraid his family might persuade him not to marry her. "I was at the mercy of Martin and his family."

And the unborn baby. "Abortion was never an option, and I'm against it to this day. But the baby is hardly even there and it's totally screwing up your whole life. I felt like it was the end of everything, my reputation and all the rest. I was planning on doing missionary service that summer, was on a solid evangelical track. And I was knocked off the track—or I put myself off the track."

Martin's parents were upset but supportive. His dad picked him up at the airport and, on the long drive home, Martin remembers having one of the best talks he has ever had with his father. After staying overnight with his parents, he flew east to Elise's home.

She met him at the airport with two friends and a knot in her gut. As they drove away the friends sat in the front seat, Elise and Martin in the back. To her relief, Martin turned to Elise and asked, "Do you want to marry me?"

They were wed a few days later, in the pastor's office, witnessed by her family and a couple of friends. Someone from the church had heard about the wedding and sent a bouquet over that morning.

Before the marriage, they spoke with the church's elders. They asked Elise to write a letter explaining her situation to the youth of the church (she had been a sponsor of the youth group), and she was banned from any leadership positions for a year. While they no longer attend the little church, Elise and Martin have warm memories of it. "They acted as a family to us."

The couple returned to school in confusion, having "honeymooned" a single night in an Econo-Lodge. The plan, as best they had it, was to finish the school year, then take a year off to have the baby. They would later return and finish their educations one at a time.

Newlywed, they arrived at the airport several miles from their school, carrying only a few dollars. They hadn't arranged for anyone to meet them, and could reach no school friends by phone. Says Martin: "There was a guy directing cabs, and he could see we needed help. He ended up driving us in this beat-up blue car—he could have lost his job for stealing a fare. He had just started reading the Bible, and he found out we were

Christians. We gave him a Bible and all the money we had. He said his name was Harry Wallet. I still wonder if he was an angel."

They slept in their separate dorm rooms that night. Then they faced the college's administration, expecting to be kicked out of school. Instead, says Martin, "It was all grace." The director of student development offered to give them pots and pans and some dishes. He saw to it that they were reimbursed dormitory and cafeteria fees for the remainder of the semester. The dean of women found a couple for them to live with for the rest of the school year. "She told us they were going to be a good example of marriage to us," Elise says.

"I remember going to meet the Lintners and feeling like scum, totally ashamed of what had happened," she continues. "And I remember Bill sitting there and talking to us so nicely. I didn't know they knew I was pregnant, and when he said, 'So, when's the baby due?' I was blown away that he would ask that so casually."

Back at school, word of the sudden marriage spread. Close friends were supportive, but other students were not. Elise recalls sitting in the library and seeing an acquaintance from home enter the building with a boyfriend. She conspicuously whispered in his ear. He looked straight at Elise and boisterously proclaimed, "Oh my God!"

For the rest of the semester, Elise departed campus as soon as classes were finished, heading directly to the shelter of the Lintners' home. She and Martin lived with them for two months.

Come summer, they moved back to Elise's hometown, found a hospital, and began planning for the baby. One

September day Elise went for an ultrasound examination. She and Martin remember the hesitancy on the part of the attendant doctors, and the repeated scanning. Finally they were told, "The doctor who reads these things isn't here now. Can you come back after lunch?"

"It was a teaching hospital," says Martin. "We thought nothing of them wanting to check with a professor."

After lunch, they waited in a hallway. A single physician appeared, stood in front of them, and said, "Your baby has no skull."

Once more, Elise remembers, there was a roaring in her ears. She had spent the summer struggling with this "interruption" in her life; only in the last few weeks had she gotten excited about the upcoming birth. Now she and Martin, surrounded by a converging party of specialists, were ushered into a conference room. There she stammered, "What do you *mean*, it has no skull?" (Eventually doctors would speculate that part of the amniotic sac had torn away and wrapped around the developing baby's head, preventing normal growth.)

It was a forty-five-minute drive to Elise's parents. Elise and Martin cried all the way, told them the news, were held and comforted on the couch, and cried some more. The next few weeks were an agonizing limbo. The doctors suspected the pressure of an ordinary, vaginal delivery would kill the baby. The only option was the radical step of laying Elise completely open, lifting the baby out, and attempting to construct a skull on the spot. It would put Elise at serious risk and still guarantee nothing for the baby.

So the young marriage was faced with another, nearly incredible burden. Elise says, "We didn't know if the baby was going to die. We didn't know if we were going to end up having a severely retarded child to take care of. We didn't know at all."

They decided against extraordinary intervention. Two weeks past the due date, physicians induced labor. Elise was in pain through the night and well into the next day. Finally, the doctors elected to perform a Cesarean section.

On November 22, 1983, Jill Elise was born. Her parents never saw her or even heard her. She was removed inconspicuously from her mother's womb. She did not cry. The nurses baptized her. Doctors and pastors decided it would be best if the young couple did not see the severely deformed child, who died within twenty-four hours. Today, although they have a healthy daughter, Amy, Martin and Elise wish they had pressed the issue.

When you ask Elise and Martin how they have come so far, through so much, they speak of grieving and growing up together. Addressing their marriage theologically, Elise is appropriately cautious. "I don't understand any of this, God's sovereignty, how such terrible things can work together for good. But sometimes I really think part of the reason our marriage made it was because of what happened. We've been through hell together. How could we separate after that?"

It has not been simple, she admits. "Because of divorce in my family, I don't have a lot of tools for thinking how relationships are supposed to stay together." They owe much, Martin says, to therapy. In the third year of their marriage, Elise felt extreme bitterness over the baby's death. Since then, she and Martin have sought counseling individually and together. They say they have learned important things about themselves. Elise: "I think we would have stayed together without it, but our marriage would not be so rich. Therapy is a manifestation of God's grace to us."

It was a therapist who suggested they have a second "wedding." She thought a black cloud hung over their marriage because they had never really celebrated it. So Martin rented a tux and they called in friends and family to reaffirm their vows. It was, in Martin's words, "a blast." Members of the party got hung up in traffic and were half an hour late, but no one fretted. This was a simple, unpressured ceremony. The invitations for it began: "Rejoicing in God's redeeming grace in their lives...."

There are other marriages in which the spouses fight less, other marriages in which the spouses got married at an older and more mature age and seem more temperamentally compatible, more "made for each other." Certainly there are other marriages in which there was no pregnancy out of wedlock and the death of a child has not been suffered.

But if Martin and Elise are still married in twenty years or so, and they expect to be, they will be the ones who can answer the question, "How can you love each other no matter what? How can you survive mistakes and sin and tragedy? How can you look for grace in everything?"

Commentary

How did it happen that Martin and Elise's marriage didn't become just another statistic?

In many ways this is not an uncommon story. Their relationship started out so well. They met at a Christian college. While they felt a strong physical attraction to each other, they tried to set clear physical boundaries. Their motives were sincere and their intentions were great, but the temptation was greater. With the sin came the inevitable confusion, shame, guilt, and depression. But Elise and Martin still cared for each other. When they came back from summer vacation they set new goals and made the decision that "sex was out of the picture." But once again, the temptation proved greater than their good intentions.

Temptation means to "put to the test"; it is one of the main weapons in Satan's arsenal against us. But what Satan has designed for evil our God can use for good. Temptation can provide the fire that can bring the alloys and impurities of our life to the surface (see 2 Pet 1:6-7). As we allow God to remove them we can become "pure gold."

Jesus warned his disciples to "watch and pray so that you will not fall into temptation. The spirit is willing, but the body is weak" (Mt 26:41). When Martin and Elise allowed themselves to be caught off guard it changed their lives. When the great king and mighty warrior David allowed himself to be caught off guard it changed the rest of his life. In 2 Samuel 11 we find that it started out so innocently. He went for a stroll on the roof of his palace and noticed Bathsheba bathing. He observed that she was a fine-looking woman. While his initial thought was not sin, he made a huge mistake: He continued to dwell on Bathsheba. He began to entertain fantasies about being with her. Soon they committed adultery.

That's the way temptation works—often a temptation to linger too long rather than to commit a sin right off. From the clear teaching of Scripture, from Martin and Elise's experience as well as from my own, I can tell you that the longer you linger the sooner you'll stumble.

Martin and Elise made a couple of choices that set them up for failure. Watching a movie like *An Officer and a Gentleman,* while not necessarily sinful, was not wise. Allowing themselves to be in a place where compromise was possible after watching the movie was even more foolish. As soon as they became aware of where they were headed they had a window of time to make another decision. If we don't *immediately* identify the impure thoughts and take those thoughts captive to what we know to be true ... if we don't *immediately* replace the wrong thinking with right thinking, we will become so weak that we don't care what we do.

In *Dancing With Broken Bones,* David Swartz has written that "temptation is the striptease of sin. In seducing our hearts, it promises satisfaction and fulfillment that never genuinely materialize in the way originally anticipated. One thing is promised, another is delivered." The price of not *immediately* "taking every thought captive to the obedience of Christ" is a price too high for any of us to pay.

Most Christians want to be strong and victorious. At the end of our life we want to hear God say, "Well done, thou good and faithful servant." We want our lives to be characterized by integrity. The problem is that each of us has blind spots, weaknesses, and deeply entrenched habits that can sabotage our best intentions. When we make mistakes, when we slip, when we fall, when we sin the next step becomes the most important one.

By God's grace Martin and Elise made a wise decision. They sought the Lord's guidance to find his will for them. The support of family and friends also made a big difference. The role of the church in helping them deal with their sin in a responsible way was followed up by demonstrations of support and encouragement. The love, acceptance, and support of their mentor couple, the Lintners, gave them a model of what a good marriage looked like.

As they were on the road to recovery and beginning to lay a strong foundation for a healthy marriage relationship, they experienced an even more painful event, the death of their precious baby, who lived only for a day. Once again, they were faced with a choice. They could focus, dwell on, and be consumed by the massive loss. Or, they could once again reach out for the support of the body of Christ and face the loss, acknowledge the grief, and, one step at a time, one day at a time, move through it. They applied the two wisdom principles they learned from the Lintners. Through the Reacquaintance Principle they got constantly reacquainted with each other through activities such as structured communication times, praying together, and dating. Through the Resolution Principle they learned the importance of addressing grievances when they arise and not allowing many little issues to become a confusing mountain of major issues that are difficult to define and challenging to resolve.

By God's grace and their choice they allowed their friends and church family to minister to them. They grieved and they grew up together. Martin had the maturity to put his wife first and cut back on his basketball games to parent Amy so that Elise could continue to work on her master's degree. In the third year they sought professional counseling, individually and as a couple.

Most people would say that their marriage survived in spite of what happened to them. The people who know them best would say that their marriage didn't merely survive ... it has *thrived* because of the ways in which they allowed God to work through their circumstances.

Resources

Doug Rosenau, *A Celebration of Sex* (Nashville, Tenn.: Thomas Nelson, 1994).

Lewis Smedes, *Sex for Christians* (Grand Rapids, Mich.: Eerdmans, 1976).

John White, *Eros Defiled* (Downers Grove, Ill.: InterVarsity, 1977).

H. Norman Wright, *So You're Getting Married* (Ventura, Calif.: Gospel Light, 1997).

Chapter 10

Emotional Infidelity
by Janis Long Harris

This story is a composite of the experiences of three people, each of whom dealt with sexual temptation in a similar way. Names, places, and other details have been changed to assure anonymity.

I've never thought of myself as the kind of man who would get romantically involved with a woman other than my wife. I'm a Christian. I know the meaning of morality. And I love my wife.

This is why my obsession with Joan took me by surprise.

I have been married to Laurie for more than ten years. We have three children and what I would describe as a relatively happy marriage. But after our third child was born, our marriage went into a slump.

Laurie had become somewhat depressed and, enmeshed in her own emotions, was ruling the house with how she felt. She put on weight and wasn't as interested in sex as she had been before. And she seemed to have become selfish, exhibiting no interest in my work, for example, even though it was very important to me.

I was thriving in my new job selling phone systems to small businesses. This was my first attempt at making it in the "real world." Having grown up in a Christian home and previously worked for a Christian organization, I had always wondered if I was "man enough" to make it in the secular world. To my surprise, I was succeeding in an extremely competitive environment.

A short time after I started my new job, I met Joan, my main contact for my most important customer. I had to meet with her at least weekly. Joan was sweet and conscientious—and, as it turned out, in the middle of a bad marriage. Her husband was a heavy drinker who abused her both emotionally and physically. I usually met Joan at a local Denny's for breakfast, and she would frequently come into the restaurant with her eyes red from a night of crying and no sleep.

I found myself feeling protective of Joan. It hurt me to see her working so hard on her marriage with nothing but pain to show for it.

At the same time, I found myself pulling away from my wife. It seemed that no matter what I did, I couldn't please her. Take the garden I was raising, for example. After working at the office all day, I'd come home, put on some jeans, and work in the rows of vegetables until late at night. But despite the fact that Laurie was always griping about the prices in the supermarket, she took no interest in this project. Instead, she just seemed to get more resentful.

Joan, on the other hand, showed a lot of interest in what I did and said. She grew up on a farm so when I told her I had just cut the first broccoli heads, she knew exactly what I was talking about. I felt like I was talking to a real friend. If I clinched a big deal at the office, Joan was like a cheerleader applauding me from the sidelines. She was genuinely happy for me. My wife was happy only because of the bonus check involved.

It got to the point that I didn't enjoy being around Laurie. Instead, I found myself yearning to see Joan. She understood when I was having trouble with an account, and she was knowledgeable about my hobbies. No matter how trivial the things I talked about, she appeared to be fascinated.

I'm sure I must have seemed like an ideal husband to Joan. I tried to be thoughtful and work hard around the house, while her husband was basically a slob who gave her a hard time about any request she might make for the smallest of household repairs.

I'll never forget the day I realized I was emotionally transferring my loyalties from my wife to Joan. I was training for a marathon and would often go out running for several hours at a time. After you've been running for more than a couple of hours, your resistance melts down and your body takes over to keep you going. After I reached that point, I found that all I could think about was Joan. Everything else would fade away. I tried to think about my wife, the kids, the garden, anything. But I couldn't concentrate for more than thirty seconds. Despite the fact that my wife is a beautiful woman, that I loved her, that I wanted our marriage to work, Joan was the image that would light up for me. No matter how hard I tried to deny it, I knew I was developing a true obsession.

I didn't do anything about it right away. After all, I told myself, Joan and I weren't really having an affair. At least, we had never actually made love. I guess if you took whatever intimacy represents and removed sex from it, that's what Joan and I had. Despite some heavy-duty temptation, we never crossed the line into a physical relationship. I was proud of myself for that.

What began to scare me, though, was my fantasy life. Even though I never considered leaving my wife, I found myself thinking about what would happen if she died. I fantasized this whole scenario about Laurie dying, about being comforted by my family, about being free to pursue Joan.

By this time I knew I could have Joan if I wanted her. Her marriage was so destructive that, if she had had something to run away to, she would have.

Surprisingly, Joan and I never talked much about our relationship. I guess we were afraid that talking about it would create barriers. We both knew there was no future for us and that there shouldn't be. So as long as we didn't talk about it, we could follow the path we were on—wherever it took us.

My obsession with Joan had been going on for about a year when I finally decided that things were out of control. I didn't trust myself to think things through rationally, so I decided to call a friend of mine, a Christian guy I used to work with. To my relief, he didn't start dropping Bible verses on me. Instead, he was sympathetic but firm.

"I can understand the attraction," he said, "but where are you going with this? You can't just let this thing float along. You have to be aware of its power. You have to make choices. Don't let this relationship control you."

I knew he was right. Not long after our conversation, I decided to ask my company for a transfer. It was the hardest thing I've ever done.

My wife is from northern California and we'd always

dreamed of moving to that area someday. Because houses are a lot more expensive there than where we were living in Seattle, we didn't think we'd be able to make the move for at least five years, maybe longer. So Laurie was probably puzzled when I started talking about moving right away.

When I told Joan, she knew immediately what it meant—the end of our future. But she didn't plead or even ask me if I was sure.

Maybe it was the coward's way out, using geography to solve my problem, but I knew I had to get away before it really got out of control. And once I made the decision, things moved pretty quickly. There happened to be an opening in California and I was gone within a month.

Before I left, I went to a trade show that Joan also attended. We were together for a week in the same hotel. It was a real test of my self-control. Every night Joan was sleeping on the same floor. My mind was all over the place. What would happen if I knocked on her door? After ten years of marriage, the thrill and exploration of sex was long gone. The exquisite tension I experienced those evenings in my hotel room was something I hadn't felt in a long time.

We never did sleep with each other. I would usually hug her good night at the end of each day and, on a couple of occasions, we even kissed. That's as far as we went physically. I left for California congratulating myself for my self-control.

I'd been gone for about a month when the situation blew apart.

Laurie and our children were staying in Seattle until we bought a new house, so I was coming back on weekends to be with them. During one of those trips back, I arranged to meet

Joan at a beach cabin my company owns. We had an idyllic afternoon together, eating lunch while watching the stunning scenery from huge windows that jutted out over the bay. Afterward, we spent three hours watching whales swim by.

I was back home that evening when the call came. It was Joan. Somehow her husband, Paul, had found out about our afternoon rendezvous. She made some excuses about business we needed to go over, but he was in a rage. And now she wanted me there with her.

She was crying. "Jim, I want you to come over right away," she said, her voice desperate.

I made a weak attempt at protest. "But, Joan, it's ten o'clock."

"I know, but I'm scared and I need you here," she pleaded. "Please come."

I told my wife some story about the computers going down at the office and took off. I was scared. Paul is a huge guy, a logger who tosses trees around for a living. His size and his violent temper made him potentially very dangerous.

I walked into Joan's house not knowing what to expect, but preparing myself for the worst. And when I walked in, I walked into a maelstrom. What followed was a blur of violent shouting and tearful pleading. Convinced that Joan and I had been having an affair, Paul was beside himself with fury.

He raged on and on, spewing out obscenities, calling me every abusive name he could think of. Every ounce of anger and resentment he'd ever felt about injustices in his life seemed to have been concentrated in this moment and he was venting it all on us with full force.

The violent scene went on until almost midnight. When I finally left, I looked over my shoulder at Joan, wondering if she would be beaten up that night. I was scared, ashamed, angry ... and relieved to still be alive. Then my survival instincts kicked in. I had to find some way out of this.

Pretty sure that Paul would call my wife, I went home and spilled out the whole story. I tried to take as much of the blame as I could, but I also told Laurie about my discontent with our marriage, about how I felt my needs weren't being met, about how my obsession with Joan had grown out of a desire for someone to listen to me and care about things that were important to me. When I stopped, our marriage was up for grabs.

For about a month, Laurie took revenge any way she could. She wouldn't sleep with me and took every opportunity to be cutting and sarcastic. I didn't know if our marriage would survive.

Although in some ways I felt I deserved her wrath, I also felt I deserved some credit for not having crossed the line into a physical relationship with Joan. Laurie was treating me as if I had had a sexual affair. There were times when I felt sorry for myself and thought, "I should have gone ahead and slept with Joan when I had the chance. At least then I would have had some memories to take with me."

After a few weeks, however, Laurie gradually began to warm up. She lost some weight and started wearing clothes she knew would please me. And she forgave me. It took about six months, but we both began to recover emotionally.

I realize now that Laurie needed that time to deal with the initial shock and pain of learning that I had been romantically involved with another woman. I had betrayed her love and her trust, and she had wanted to punish me.

But to her credit, Laurie decided that prolonging the emotional cold war wasn't the best way to deal with the situation. So gradually, as she saw that I was being faithful to her and to our relationship, she decided to approach this as an opportunity to address the weaknesses in our marriage. We both began to work for positive change. (I never saw Joan or Paul again, but I heard later that they got a divorce.)

Looking back, I'd say our marriage is stronger for having gone through this ordeal. Having said that, there are question marks of trust in Laurie's mind that probably will never go away. When I'm traveling, she quizzes me every time I call in. I can tell she's thinking, "I wonder who's in the room next to him now?"

I also bear a lot of guilt about the breakup of Joan's marriage. Although there probably wasn't much there to save, our relationship put her in the position of taking the rap. Her husband blames her for ruining the marriage. Before our relationship, she could have said, "This is a dangerous marriage and I need to get out of it." Afterward, she was the guilty party. She was the one who flirted with adultery. I worry about her being tormented by guilt.

Joan's husband, of course, will probably never darken the door of a church again. One of the main reasons he'll give is that guys like me who are supposed to be Christians are really just like everybody else. So my dalliance with infidelity had some serious costs.

I learned a few things from this experience, though. I don't spend as much time worrying about having a marriage that's perfect in every way. I've settled into a different level of contentment. I've learned to give up the fantasy of having it all. I don't let the "what-ifs" and "if-onlys" dominate my life the way they used to.

I've also learned to get my needs met in appropriate ways. If I define my needs as companionship, intimacy, and someone to care about me—yet only pick women to meet those needs—I'm putting myself in a dangerous situation. So I've made a point of cultivating male friendships, friendships that allow for deep sharing.

I'm also better at recognizing the dynamics that are likely to get me into the same situation I was in with Joan. I still believe my original motives were pure. Any Christian who saw Joan coming to work hurt would have wanted to comfort and protect her. But in my case, those protective instincts got out of hand. So when another woman at work confided that her husband was an alcoholic, instead of trying to counsel her myself, suggested she join Al-Anon to get the help she needed.

I don't fully understand what Jesus meant when he said that lusting after a woman is the same thing as adultery, but I know I lusted after Joan. Even though we never had sex, there's a sense in which we did commit adultery. Even though ours was an affair of the mind, it was an affair nonetheless.

If I had an opportunity to give advice to someone else who was struggling with a "mental affair," I'd say: Even though my wife and I were able to redeem our marriage, you don't know what's going to happen to yours. You don't know when your outside relationship is going to start controlling you instead of the other way around.

My relationship with Joan was exciting. But deep down, I knew my wife, my kids, and my marriage covenant before God were more important. I couldn't take the risk of throwing all that away.

As my friend said, you have to make choices. With God's help, I made the right one.

Commentary

On any given day thousands of different thoughts cross our minds. Some are good, some are neutral, and some are bad. Do you ever have thoughts enter your mind that make you wonder where they came from? Have you ever been in prayer and suddenly been aware of a bitter, or angry, or selfish, or lustful thought? You're not alone. In fact, I've yet to meet a person who didn't answer "yes" to those questions.

That's the kind of situation that Jim faced. He and Laurie had been married for ten years and had a relatively happy marriage. After the birth of their third child their marriage went into a slump. That's not uncommon. Many couples experience a decrease in their marriage satisfaction after the birth of a child. While a birth is a blessed event, it can often create some relational rapids for a couple to navigate.

Jim allowed his unhealthy focus on his own needs to obscure his opportunity to practice 1 Corinthians 13 and Ephesians 5:21-33. He let his mind wander, and his heart followed. The good news is that he didn't enter into a sexual relationship with Joan, and finally reached out and called a Christian friend for advice. Fortunately, this friend didn't go to the same school of counseling that Job's friends had. He didn't dump Bible verses on him. He listened. He cared. He spoke the truth in love and he reminded Jim of the power of choices.

Each of us needs to ask God to help us determine moral choices. If it's not something that is clearly spelled out in Scripture, pray about it and seek the counsel of several wise friends. *Always* leave yourself a margin. If God has told you not to go beyond the fifty-yard line, don't tiptoe up to the forty-nine yard, two-feet, and eleven-inch mark. Don't see how close you can get to the line without going over it. That's about as smart as a scuba diver seeing how little air he can leave in his tank and still get to the surface.

Fortunately Jim and Laurie's story has a happy ending. Jim made a wise decision. He decided to run. Was this the coward's way out? What do you think? When Joseph was confronted by Potiphar's wife, he ran. In 1 Corinthians 6:18 Paul tells us to run from sexual immorality. In 2 Timothy 2:22 we're told to run from the evil desires of youth. Sounds like good advice to me. When in doubt, run. When you have a question, run. When you are tempted to compromise, run.

Jim made a good move but he didn't have the support and the plan to stick with it. He made the same discovery that almost every other man (or woman) who has been suckered into the same deceptive scenario has made, not realizing that the passion that comes from a fantasy relationship is hard to let go of. Jim compromised his commitment with a rendezvous at the beach cabin owned by his company. By God's grace the call from Joan's husband turned into a wake-up call for Jim.

When he told Laurie, her response was a normal one. She felt betrayed, she felt hurt, she was devastated, and she took revenge any way she could. But over a six-month period Laurie made an important decision. She chose to forgive and the healing was able to begin. Jim tells us that he learned some painful but powerful lessons. He learned not to expect a perfect marriage, to dump the silly fantasy of having it all, to ignore the seduction of the "what-ifs," and to get his needs met in healthy ways. He also learned the importance of cultivating male friendships.

"Whoever can be trusted with very little can also be trusted with much, and whoever is dishonest with very little will also be dishonest with much" (Lk 16:10).

One of the major lessons we can learn from failure is that there are no little things. The majority of the mistakes and failures in my life haven't been major or catastrophic. Most of them have been small and seemingly insignificant. Most often they didn't involve sin—only laziness, poor judgment, or compromise.

But these "little things" set me up for and made me more vulnerable to other decisions that got me a bit further from the "straight and narrow." The problem wasn't in my initial decisions. The problem was the direction these decisions took me in and the perspective they robbed me of. A series of small and subtle five-degree changes can eventually lead to behaviors that will turn into failure.

Satan knows it will be hard to get us to do an about-face. But he can get us to veer off the road. And then he can talk us into taking a "harmless" detour. He can talk us into believing that "it's not that bad." And he knows that if he can get us even slightly off course, if he can get us to take our eyes off our Lord, if he can seduce us into believing we can do it on our own, he has won a major victory. That's why it is so important to cultivate the habit of being faithful in little. If you learn how to be faithful in the "little" you won't have to worry about the "much."

Resources

Laurie Hall, *An Affair of the Mind* (Colorado Springs, Colo: Focus on the Family, 1996).

Charles Milander, *Running the Red Lights* (Ventura, Calif.: Regal, 1986).

Doug Rosenau, *A Celebration of Sex* (Nashville, Tenn.: Thomas Nelson, 1994).

John White, *Eros Defiled* (Downers Grove, Ill.: InterVarsity, 1977).

Earl Wilson, *Sexual Sanity* (Downers Grove, Ill.: InterVarsity, 1984).

Chapter 11

Pornography
by James D. Berkley

*W*hile we hear from counselors that this problem is increasingly prevalent, it's rare that a couple is willing to talk about it. But with the hope of helping other couples who are struggling, Steve and Beth Patterson (not their real names) tell their story with amazing candor. With God's help, they are rebuilding their marriage and moving beyond Steve's sexual addiction.

Steve: My problems with pornography began in sixth grade. My dad was supposed to bring something home for me from his office. I opened his briefcase and found a copy of *Playboy* instead. I took the magazine to my mom, who told me, "Oh, someone just gave that to your dad. He doesn't really look at it." But the idea of those pictures stayed with me, and the next time I was alone in the house, I searched Dad's closet and found another magazine. Then every time my parents went out, I'd search out a *Playboy* and look at it.

I had always been the all-American kid—well liked, good at

sports, the whole nine yards. But I felt a real burden to be that "perfect" kid—to live up to everyone else's expectations. In many ways, I was lonely. My parents were busy with work and with my siblings. I think I used sexual fantasies as an escape, like some people resort to drugs or alcohol.

For years I thought I might be sexually abnormal because I was so drawn to sexual images. Now I understand that looking at those pictures was my first experience ever with sex—powerful stuff for a kid in the sixth grade. Most boys growing up see a *Playboy* or something like it sooner or later, but some kids keep going back to it. And it becomes more than simply looking at exciting pictures. For me, it was a way to deal with pain and disappointment.

Beth: Steve played the role of the perfect man. In fact, he was so good in this role that I sometimes thought he had a lower sex drive than most men because he seemed almost *disinterested* in it. When we were dating, one of the things that endeared Steve to me was the fact that he was a virgin. And once we were married, I cherished the fact that we had been only with each other. It never entered my mind to suspect that he was addicted to pornography.

Steve: The fact is, no normal guy is "disinterested" in sex. My secret life with pornography was a powerful contradiction to the perfect-person role I was playing. I couldn't be honest about my consuming interest in sex, so I played the ultimate Puritan. Around the time we got married, I even picketed—with Beth and others—outside a local porn store.

Actually, my involvement with pornography fluctuated. In

high school, it was limited to looking at my dad's copies of *Playboy*. In college, I didn't feel the pull so much, maybe because I was excited about dating Beth. And then for the first few months we were married, pornography wasn't a problem.

But eventually Beth and I started running into some problems, the kind that are typical in marriage. But they were intimidating to me. I was still trying to be the all-American perfect guy and I couldn't admit any faults. I was more accustomed to retreating from problems than to dealing with them.

Beth: Looking back, I can see there were warning signs that I didn't know how to read. For example, I used to complain to Steve that I never felt "one" with him. He was often distant, distracted—and he wouldn't tell me what he was thinking about. Or he'd be angry, and I couldn't understand what was making him mad. Also, our sex life was mediocre; Steve never seemed to have a pressing need for physical intimacy.

Steve: How could I be one with Beth? My secret affected all my relationships. I never could be myself because if people found out how I *really* was, my cover would be blown. I felt I had to protect myself.

Faced with an unhappy marriage that he didn't know how to deal with, Steve fell back on a pattern he had developed in childhood. Rather than face his problems head-on and try to solve them, he relieved the pressures he was feeling by seeking out the fantasy world of pornography.

Steve: One day at work another guy was getting ready to go on a trip. He flashed a pornographic magazine at me and teased, "Look what I've got!"

My first thought was, "No. I don't want to look at that." But I had never really dealt with my pornography problem, and that incident planted a seed. I couldn't get the image out of my mind, so I decided I would buy just one magazine.

Then my addiction kicked in. I started buying a lot more than just one *Playboy*. The more I got into it, the more I felt that the material had to be stronger, more explicit. I started getting videos. I even called some of those telephone dial-a-porn lines.

I was a salesman, on the road calling on clients. My sales territory was small, so most days I didn't have enough to do. Frequently, I filled my time with pornography. Beth never saw the magazines I purchased because almost immediately I'd become disgusted with myself and get rid of them before I went home. Plus I handled all our family finances so Beth wouldn't see any evidence of my spending.

Beth: I started blaming myself for our troubled marriage. I always thought Steve was mad at me, and I felt responsible for his lack of desire for me. I thought it was *my* fault Steve was so distant.

Steve: I was trapped in a cycle with pornography: I'd throw it all out, then I'd buy more. Then I'd throw *that* out, only to go and buy more. Over and over I confessed my sin to God and asked for forgiveness. But a few days after praying, I'd be back at it. I went to unfamiliar churches to try to find a pastor to talk with anonymously. I even tried to get through to TV preachers.

If I'd really wanted to, I could have found help. But my craving had taken control of my life. And since I thought there was no way I could tell Beth, I tried to work it through myself.

And all along, the "thrill" that I got from my episodes with pornography never outweighed the guilt and frustration I experienced over it. I'd think, "Gosh, why do I keep doing this?" But that's how addiction is. If I could've stopped it with rational thinking, I would have. But shame had become a habit, and all the shame I felt just seemed to drive me to more and more pornography.

There were times when Beth said, "Steve, is there something you should tell me?" or, "What are you hiding?" I'd feel my face get red. I'd answer, "Nothing," and I'd pray, "God, don't let this come out until I've gotten it taken care of."

Beth: About six years into our marriage, soon after our son was born, our finances got messed up. Steve had always handled all our money. In fact, he'd go to the mailbox before me to get the credit card bill. (I realized later he was doing that so I wouldn't see charges for calls he had made to dial-a-porn numbers and bills from an adult bookstore.) We started getting calls from bill collectors. Since I'd never seen the bills, I had no idea our debt was heavily connected with pornography. But I could see that dealing with the family finances seemed to make Steve extremely depressed, so I offered to take it over.

Steve: I felt so defeated that I was almost ready to let Beth handle our money. I figured if she was in charge of the bills, it would force me to stop buying the trash. I resolved to make another new beginning, and for three weeks I was clean. I had to stay off the stuff so Beth wouldn't see any charges on our current bills when I turned them over to her.

I was starting to fool myself into believing that I had really quit, and the thought occurred to me, "Boy, wouldn't it be horrible if she found out now—right when I'm getting this problem under control?" That very day I called home from work just to say hello, and discovered that Beth had found out the horrible truth.

Beth: I was trying to figure out how far behind we were on our giving to the church. Instead, I found a stack of checks written to a store that's known for selling pornography. All at once I could see what had been going on, and it was devastating. It's like my heart broke at that moment. I actually fell down, and I cried out to God because I felt so lost.

I was holding those checks in my hand when Steve called. I asked him, "What did you buy at that store?"

He said, "Something ... not good."

And then I asked, "How many times?" because I was holding four checks in my hand.

He told me, "Once."

And I said, "Do you want to tell me the truth?" He got off the phone and came home. I called our pastor while Steve was on his way. Our pastor had become a Christian out of a worldly past. His own life had been changed, so I thought he'd be understanding and he was.

Steve: I was scared and ashamed. I couldn't believe my secret was out. But our pastor's prayer and support meant a lot, as did the support of Beth's parents. We had to tell them since Beth really needed help just then—and not from me.

Beth: My first impulse was to take our baby and get out. I didn't know whether I would stay with Steve or leave him, so I went to my parents' house for the night. I was shattered. I think I could have handled Steve's death better than such a betrayal.

This just didn't fit my picture of Steve. Here he'd had all these cravings and fantasies that I knew nothing about! And not just a fleeting lapse—it was long-term perversion.

After that first night, I went back home to Steve, but emotionally, I wasn't with him. I was dragging my feet in getting back into our relationship emotionally. But I knew God wanted us to stay married, so I finally started trying to reconnect with Steve and to support and encourage him.

At first, I couldn't believe that Steve could love me and be interested in pornography at the same time. I felt there had to be something wrong with me that made him look at all these sexually explicit pictures. I'm starting to understand better now, but I don't think a woman can ever really understand how strong that visual pull of sexuality is for guys.

Beyond the damaging addiction, trust had also been broken. After the initial discovery, I continued to uncover new details. For instance, I was about to call Visa to get our financial statements in order, and Steve stopped me to tell me about other pornography-related charges that he knew I'd find out about. To realize that he was still holding back details of his obsession really upset me.

Steve: It was difficult having Beth know about my problem, and it was hard to face her parents after they found out. But

Beth's parents showed a lot of understanding and love. I think her father was more angry about our financial trouble than about the pornography. He could see that by indulging in this addiction, I wasn't taking care of my wife and son. Our baby was sick, and we didn't have insurance or money to take him to a doctor. I had wasted about $5,000 on pornography, and now my wife and child were suffering.

Beth: Right about that time, Steve got laid off from his job. Because our finances were in such a mess, we weren't able to stay in our house even one more month. We had no money in the bank to pay our mortgage, so we sold the house.

I had wanted our family to be a solid unit, protected by God. We prayed over the house when we moved in. We hoped to be a witness to our neighbors. We wanted our son to be raised in a home where he knew Christ and learned Christian values. It felt like suddenly our protective skin had been gashed open, and all the world's evil had poured in. Steve had given himself over to everything I desperately wanted to protect our family from.

The Pattersons sought help right away. They rejected the advice of the first psychologist they saw, who told Steve to "wean" himself from pornography slowly. Steve felt sure he needed to quit immediately and permanently, with God's help. He joined a men's group for awhile, and both he and Beth have worked together with a pastoral counselor on the issues of Steve's perfectionism, their self-esteem problems, and the task of rebuilding trust between them.

Beth: Now and then I still deal with a sense of betrayal, and I have to make it a point to trust Steve. Both of us have been growing steadily, and our growth is always related to what we're doing spiritually. When we are obeying God and being truthful and honest with each other, we improve greatly. But when one of us gets out of step, our marriage takes a nosedive.

Steve: The pace of our recovery hasn't always been in sync. Men can be kind of impatient. We begin to think: "Look, the problem's out on the table, so let's pray about it and move on." But I needed to take time to work through it with Beth. Even though I just wanted to be done with the whole thing, Beth was only beginning to deal with her hurt. A week after all this came out, she was still devastated. But I was happy because I felt like a huge weight had been lifted from me.

One example is the day I got picked up by a tow truck because our car broke down. The driver had an explicit picture of a woman right on the dashboard. I couldn't help but see it. I found myself looking at it a moment too long, but I caught myself and stopped. To me it felt like a real victory.

Beth: Steve came home and told me that he had looked at that picture a bit longer than he should have, and I blew up in anger. Part of the reason was that he obviously felt good about looking away, while I was still reeling from hurt. But later I realized that in a forty-minute drive, Steve had glanced at the picture only once. And I admired him for being able to tell me about it. That kind of accountability leads to growth.

I'm not saying that I think husbands should always come home and say, "Well, honey, I looked at a woman with lust in my heart today." Too many details can cause a lot of strife. But I do advise being spiritually accountable to someone—a close friend, a pastor, a counselor. Once others became aware of Steve's problem, he was motivated to work hard not to disappoint them. A person with Steve's kind of addiction can't quit on his own, he needs to tell someone, and he needs to get help.

Steve: Still, a man with my problem needs some degree of accountability to his wife. It would have been extremely hard for me to have told Beth early on that I had a problem with pornography. But if I had gone ahead and done that, it would have built trust between us instead of destroying it. The best path is honesty: Tell your wife about your struggles and deal with the consequences. Terrible secrets will always find a way to get out.

Beth: We feel that when this wound finally burst open, it was the beginning of the healing of our marriage. We had more problems than simply Steve's obsession with pornography, of course. But that was the roadblock that kept us from working on other things.

Steve: It's incredible what you'll rationalize when you're addicted. But once I saw the devastation I'd caused in our marriage, that changed everything. I loved Beth; I didn't ever want to hurt her like that again. I wanted to keep my family, and that was great motivation to change.

The first three or four months were the hardest for struggling with temptation. And even now I wouldn't say my addiction has disappeared; it's simply under control. If I were to buy a pornographic magazine today and look through it, I'd be in deep trouble.

I'm learning to depend on God's help. It's a constant choosing not to pursue those fantasies.

Beth: Every night I'd pray: "God, let me know when I'm not acting right." Prayer was the one thing I knew was right. When I first found out about Steve's addiction, right away I prayed. Somehow, God helped me know that only he could get us through this.

I had to remember that Steve's sin didn't make it OK for me to sin, too. My own attitudes and emotions were in terrible shape. If some sensitive man had come along and shown sympathy, it wouldn't have taken much for me to write off my whole marriage.

At first I thought, "I don't know if I can ever have sex with Steve again." But God created a need in me, and it wasn't long before we were back together again sexually. I needed Steve to need me sexually; I wanted us to have a healthy, beautiful sexual life.

Steve: Beth did a lot of things that helped me. I remember being with her parents only a week after they'd learned about my problem. I felt like the worst person in the world. Beth was still hurt, but she hugged me anyway. I broke down when she did that. After angry words and everything else, she was—and still is—very gracious and persevering.

It helped that Beth was interested in me spiritually. She could sense when I was having trouble and would encourage me to go to God again. Also, we read a book, *Journey Toward*

Wholeness by Donald Crossland, about sexual healing. That book helped Beth understand a man's perspective on sex a little more, and I learned that there are lots of factors involved with a pornography addiction—things like issues being hidden from one another and hurts left over from childhood.

Beth: Steve was doing a lot of things right. Even his words helped. I needed to hear him say, "I love you; I don't want to lose you."

I was thankful that he *wanted* to change. How many men would—or could—truly make an about-face? Steve did. He stopped his pornographic activity, absolutely. If he hadn't, I don't think we'd be here today as a couple.

Still, several months after the initial blowup, I was in a major depression, even suicidal. The one thing that kept me from losing it was our baby. Steve was doing better, but I was despairing—and that was due to a lack of trust in God. I was losing hope when there really *was* hope.

It was clear that things were already getting better in our marriage. But my expectations were way too high. I expected a new life with Steve right away. I had a normal, but dangerously wrong, attitude that Steve should be even more apologetic and more grateful that I was still there.

Finally, I heard a Christian retreat speaker say, "Whatever is on your plate right now is there because God has given it to you." I thought, "God's given me this?" I had complained that trouble had come to me unjustly. I never thought that God might have allowed it for his own purposes. Suddenly I wanted to do better with what God had given us.

Steve: Today we can see ways we've both changed, ways our life is better now, having gone through this. I'm living in truth now; I'm not hiding. I'm generally more happy. There really is freedom in Christ, and I'm experiencing it. All the emotions I wanted to feel, all the things I wanted to be for Beth and our son, I can experience now.

My pastor says the mind is like a glass of muddy water. The only way to make it clean is to put it under the tap and run pure water into it until all the dirty water overflows. It takes awhile, but eventually the clean water is all that's left.

Commentary

Almost every sex addict can trace pornography exposure to childhood. The average age of exposure used to be eleven, but with the Internet, television, and open discussions of events such as Bill Clinton's Oval Office activities the average age is now seven. Steve followed the textbook pathway to becoming trapped in an addiction.

Patrick Carnes describes sexual addiction as "the athlete's foot of the mind." It never goes away. It always is asking to be scratched, promising relief. To scratch, however, is to cause pain and to intensify the itch.

Dr. Gerald May has written that from a spiritual perspective, "addiction is a deep-seated form of idolatry. The objects of our addictions become our false gods. These are what we worship, what we attend to, where we give our time and energy, instead of love" (*Addiction and Grace* [San Francisco: Harper, 1988], 13).

No sin is a private sin that affects only you. In fact, one of the greatest myths that leads the addict to repeat sexual behaviors is that it does not adversely affect other relationships.

The observable symptoms for a sexual addict include: preoccupation with sexual behaviors, escalating patterns of sexual activity, acting distant or withdrawn, a pattern of out-of-control behavior, inability to stop despite adverse consequences, ongoing desire or effort to limit sexual behavior, sexual obsession and fantasy as a primary coping strategy, increasing amounts of sexual experience because the current level of activity is no longer sufficient, severe mood changes around sexual activity, and the neglect of important social, occupational, or recreational activities because of sexual behavior.

The predictably downward spiral of sexual addiction can lead from printed pornography to videos, adult nightclubs, massage parlors, sex with a consenting partner, prostitution, exhibitionism and voyeurism, involuntary sexual contact, obscene phone calls, bestiality, rape, incest, and child molestation. Steve was fortunate that his sexual addiction was dealt with before it took him all the way down.

Here are seven straightforward steps that I've seen God use to help men and women move beyond good intentions, and get them on the path to purity.

Step 1: Make a decision. Almost every day you will come to some kind of fork in the road. What you decide at that point will be greatly influenced by the choices you made the day before as to the kind of person you are.

Step 2: Choose to plant good seed. Any sexual addict will tell you that it's not easy to try to be pure in an impure world. Even if you become a cultural ostrich and avoid all movies, listen only to Christian radio, read only Christian books and magazines, you are still going to struggle. You will never become a godly person by negation, by merely avoiding everything.

If a farmer doesn't plant seed in the ground, he will never harvest a crop. It doesn't matter how "weed-free" his ground is. As a farmer harvests a crop by planting good seed, you can reap a harvest of purity and integrity by planting the good seed of God's Word into your life every day, preferably in the morning.

Step 3: Determine where the line is, and then stay a safe distance away from it. Moral failure is rarely the result of a blowout. Almost always it's the result of a slow leak. Some men start with the healthy desire to provide for their families and end up becoming workaholics. Other men start with something as seemingly innocent as lingering too long over the swimsuit issue *of Sports Illustrated* or the latest Victoria's Secret catalog.

Once you have determined your limits, walk ten yards back and make that your line! *Always* leave yourself a margin. Don't see how close you can get to the line without going over it.

Step 4: Guard your heart. Moral and ethical purity start in the heart. Only the passionate love of purity can save a man from impurity. Proverbs tells us, "Guard your affections, because they influence everything else in your life."

Step 5: Guard your mind. In St. Louis there is a large railroad switchyard. The thinnest piece of steel directs a train away from one main track on to another. If you follow each track, you will find that one ends in San Francisco and the other in New York.

Our thought life is like that. What we choose to think about early in the day can determine the rest of it. Just a small deviation from God's standard can put us at risk and lead us far afield from our intended and desired destination. A spiritual war is occurring in your life, and the battlefield is your mind.

Step 6: Guard your eyes. Joseph was smart enough to know you can't play with fire and not get burned (see Gn 39). Job said, "I [have] made a covenant with my eyes" (Job 31:1). David didn't guard his eyes and ended up committing adultery with Bathsheba and murdering her husband.

Step 7: Guard the little things. Christ said, "Whoever can be trusted with very little can also be trusted with much" (Lk 16:10). In the process of becoming a godly person there are no "little" things. In fact, it's how we handle the seemingly little things that over time determine our response to the big things.

If you or someone you love is struggling with some of the symptoms of sexual addiction I would encourage you to give them this story to read. Then refer them to one of the resources below and give them the name of a pastor or Christian counselor who understands the course and treatment for sexual addiction. Remind them that there is help and there is hope.

Resources

Patrick Carnes, *Don't Call It Love: Recovery from Sexual Addiction* (New York: Bantam, 1992).

——, *Out of the Shadows: Understanding Sexual Addiction* (Center City, Minn.: Hazelden Foundation, 1992).

Mark Laaser, *Faithful and True: Sexual Integrity in a Fallen World* (Nashville, Tenn.: LifeWay, 1996).

——, *The Secret Sin: Healing the Wounds of Sexual Addiction* (Grand Rapids, Mich.: Zondervan, 1992).

Gary J. Oliver, *Made Perfect in Weakness: The Amazing Things God Can Do With Failure* (Colorado Springs, Colo.: Chariot Victor, 1995).

Chapter 12

Children With Disabilities
by Susan Shelley

I lay flat on my back, just moments after giving birth to our third child, a daughter named Mandy. The intense pain of childbirth was mingled with relief that the labor and delivery were over. I wanted to rest, but first I wanted to hold my baby.

"We need to measure that head," the doctor said.

"Why?" I heard my husband, Marshall, ask. "Is something wrong?"

I couldn't hear the reply, but the doctor's voice was calm so I wasn't alarmed. He said something about "possible microcephaly," but that term was meaningless to me. I was concentrating on seeing and holding our daughter, and she looked perfect.

After several moments, Mandy was taken away, and I was wheeled to the recovery room. Marshall left for the airport to get his mother. Before he could get back, the doctor stopped by the maternity ward.

"Your daughter has a condition called microcephaly," he

said. "That means she has a small brain. Normal head circumference is thirty-five centimeters, and hers is thirty-one centimeters." He went on to say that some people with microcephaly live normal lives, while others have mental limitations.

My brain was still cloudy. I didn't understand what he was talking about. *Small head. Was this dwarfism?* I recalled being told that one of my relatives had such a small head he couldn't find hats that fit. Was that related?

But when the doctor talked about possible retardation, I began to panic. *Why isn't Marshall here? There's something wrong with our baby, and he's off being a responsible son when I need him here!* My husband's absence during that traumatic moment was only the first of many strains that the next two years would place on our marriage and our trust in God.

For the first few weeks, we prayed that Mandy would be "normal." But we eventually realized that her retardation was severe and profound: she would never talk, walk, sit up, or use her hands. She suffered frequent seizures, and soon we were squirting three different medications down her throat.

When Mandy was three months old, her doctor discovered cataracts clouding both her eyes. She had surgery to remove them, but even with her thick glasses we never knew if she could see. Neither did we know if she could hear. She didn't turn her head to the sound of my voice the way our other babies had. The only time we saw her respond to stimuli was when her body occasionally would relax in a warm bath.

Suddenly, our family life revolved around Mandy's care. She endured a series of pneumonias and *status epilepticus* (prolonged seizures), all of which were life-threatening. Virtually every month she had to be hospitalized. With our lifestyle of ongoing emergencies and frequent trips to medical facilities, Marshall jokingly called them "our Club Med vacations."

"Usually when you face a crisis, it demands your full attention and then is resolved—happily or not," Marshall said. "But this emergency just goes on and on."

We soon learned of the danger this ongoing crisis posed for our marriage. Couples with a seriously handicapped child have an 80 percent divorce rate, we were told. We determined not to become one of the statistics, but we experienced enough of the tensions to recognize the danger.

Much of the conflict in our marriage arose from the different ways Marshall and I handled the strain. I threw myself into Mandy's care, monitoring and administering her medications at the proper times. Marshall took turns bathing, medicating, and feeding her, but I was the one who posted the charts and consulted with the doctors to adjust dosages.

When her muscles became contracted, I took her for weekly physical therapy at a nearby Easter Seals center. I developed a whole new set of friends who were involved in caring for handicapped kids. Marshall never met them since he was working during the afternoons we went.

Mandy always had difficulty eating—sometimes it would take eight hours to get her to swallow four ounces of formula. I would keep at it. Again, Marshall would help, but he found it hard to sit for more than an hour trying to feed Mandy.

Most demanding, when she couldn't sleep at night— restlessly squirming and groaning—I would hold her, sitting in our rocker/recliner all night, eventually dozing off with Mandy in my arms. After several nights of this each week, I suffered from sleep deficit. Marshall never awoke when Mandy was squirmy; I couldn't sleep when she was restless.

If we had to make a middle-of-the-night run to the emergency room, Marshall would willingly go while I stayed home with our other two girls, but the burden of Mandy's care fell to me. While my husband was supportive, I felt lonely. One evening I was crying, overwhelmed by our baby's situation. Marshall sat quietly next to me on the couch.

"Why don't you cry? Don't you care?" I asked him.

"Yes, I care. And I don't know why the tears don't come," he said. "Sometimes I wish I could cry, but I can't."

If he really cared, why wasn't he more visibly upset? His emotional detachment bothered me. At the dinner table, I often wanted to talk about Mandy, and Marshall would listen for awhile. But then he'd change the subject to church, or an upcoming vacation, or to one of our other girls.

Once, after I'd been on the phone with a friend, weeping about Mandy's latest setback, he said, "I'm glad you can talk with Julie. She's a great listener. But do you think she ever gets tired of hearing about Mandy's problems?"

"What do you mean?" I said. "I need to talk things out. I can't just bottle them up the way you do. I have to process them, and it takes me longer than it seems to take you."

"You know what scares me even more than Mandy's seizures?" Marshall said. "I fear people will consider us lepers. If our suffering is all we talk about, even our friends may shy away from us. We need to be honest about our situation, but maybe we shouldn't dwell on it so much in conversations. Who wants to be with someone who's depressing all the time?"

I couldn't compartmentalize life like that. At times,

Marshall's "coping by thinking of other things" angered me. I feared we weren't connecting emotionally.

His equilibrium, however, did have one benefit. Since Mandy had difficulty swallowing, her medications and formula often had to be administered through a tube that was inserted through her nose and down her throat into her stomach. I always had trouble doing that. But Marshall learned how to lubricate and gently insert the tube. What made me squeamish seemed much easier for him. After that, I began to notice the different ways he showed his concern. He took care of Mandy's almost-daily enemas and the subsequent cleanup.

My husband provided a sense of normalcy for our other two daughters. While I focused on Mandy, Marshall coached Stacey's and Kelsey's tee-ball teams and provided bike rides and trips to the arcade or to Dairy Queen. And he made sure our family always had a vacation planned that we could look forward to.

Also, his work was a means of providing for Mandy. I realized that without his job, Mandy's care wouldn't be paid for—and if he lost his job, she would be virtually uninsurable. What I had viewed as him being overly focused on work was actually his way of providing care for Mandy.

"Mandy makes me feel so helpless," he once admitted. "I can't do anything to change her condition." So he concentrated on the areas where he *could* do something.

It took us more than a year to fully understand the different roles we were playing. One day as we were discussing it, he put it this way: "Mothers often focus on their neediest child. And we've needed you to concentrate on Mandy's care. I see a dad's role as looking out for the whole family."

Suddenly, into the midst of our ongoing crisis, another surprise landed. I was pregnant again, and I was thrilled when, a few months later, the doctor told me our baby-to-be was a boy. I decided to keep that news a secret because I wanted to see Marshall's face when our son was delivered.

I did tell one of my closest friends, and she rejoiced with me. "This is God's way of honoring you for your faithfulness with Mandy," she said. It felt good to feel God's smile again.

But because of Mandy's condition we wanted to be ready in case this child also had complications. In the fifth month, our doctor recommended a Level II ultrasound. As I lay on the examining table, Dr. Silver manipulated the ultrasound, measuring the cranium and the femur and viewing the internal organs. We all watched the embryonic motions.

"Is everything OK?" Marshall asked.

"Let me complete the examination, and I'll give you a full report," the doctor said. I hoped his evasive answer was merely his standard procedure.

Moments later, Dr. Silver announced his observations in a matter-of-fact voice. "We have some problems. The fetus has a malformed heart—the aorta is attached incorrectly. There are missing portions of the cerebellum. A club foot. A cleft palate and perhaps a cleft lip. Possibly spina bifida. This is probably a case of Trisomy 13 or Trisomy 18. In either case, it is a condition incompatible with life."

Neither Marshall nor I could say anything, so Dr. Silver continued.

"It's likely the fetus will spontaneously miscarry. If the child is born, it will not survive long outside the womb. You need to decide if you want to try to carry this pregnancy to term."

We both knew what he was asking. My soul was shaken by the news, but I knew clearly what I was to do.

"God is the giver and taker of life," I said. "If the only opportunity I have to know this child is in my womb, I don't want to cut that time short. If the only world he is to know is the womb, I want that world to be as safe as I can make it."

I was shattered. When I told one friend the news, she put her arm around me and said, "Remember that God loves you."

I nodded, but inside I was screaming, "Then why doesn't he show it? This is the strangest way to express love I've ever seen!"

Summer turned to fall, and we were praying that our son would be healed. But if a long life were not God's intention for him, we prayed that he could at least experience the breath of life.

Even that request seemed in jeopardy as labor began November 22. As the contractions got more severe, signs of fetal distress caused the nurses to ask, "Should we try to deliver the baby alive?"

"Yes, if at all possible, short of surgery," I replied.

They kept repositioning me and giving me oxygen, and the fetal distress eased. And then suddenly the baby was out. The doctor cut the cord and gently placed our son on my chest. He was a healthy pink, and we saw his chest rise and fall. The breath of life. Thank you, God.

Then, almost immediately, he began to turn blue. We stroked his face and whispered words of welcome, of love, of farewell. Two minutes later, the doctor said, "He's gone."

Within moments, our pastor, our parents, and our children came into the room. Together we wept, held one another and took turns holding our son. My chest ached from heaviness. Death is enormous, immense, unstoppable.

The loss was crushing, but mingled with the tears and the terrible pain was something else. At the births of my three daughters, I'd felt "the miracle of birth," that sacred moment when a new life enters the world of light and air. The breath of life fills the lungs for the first time. Now this moment was doubly intense because the miracle of birth was followed so quickly by the mystery of death.

"Do you have a name for the baby?" asked one of the nurses.

"Toby," I said, "from a name in the Bible, Tobiah, which means 'God is good.'"

Marshall and I didn't particularly feel goodness at that moment. The name was what we *believed*, not what we felt. It was what we wanted to feel again someday.

Four days later, we loaded Toby's tiny casket into the back of our minivan and drove 750 miles to the church cemetery near my childhood home in Kansas. We didn't know then that we'd be coming back in just a few months.

Two weeks before her second birthday, Mandy developed a severe pneumonia. Despite our prayers and the physicians' treatments, after five days I began to fear we would never bring her home from the hospital. On Thursday afternoon, Marshall and I sat in Mandy's room, taking turns holding her. A procession of people stopped by to visit:

- Marshall's boss, who said, "I don't have anything to say. I just sensed I needed to be near Mandy." He told us about the loss of a loved one several years earlier. Then he left.
- A hospital volunteer, supposedly there to comfort us, who

suddenly poured out the story of her own divorce, remarriage, and feeling of estrangement from God. Now she had a desire to renew her relationship with him.

- A nurse, who uncharacteristically broke into tears and told us of growing up in a boarding school, away from her missionary parents, and never feeling close to them (or to God). But now, after caring for Mandy, she longed to regain intimacy with both her heavenly and earthly fathers.

I sat there amazed. In the presence of a dying child, a child who couldn't speak, we had a small "revival." People were coming to Mandy's room to confess sins and draw nearer to God.

At 7 P.M. Mandy left her "earthly tent" for one "not made by human hands." Amid the sorrow, we planned her funeral and drove her tiny casket the same 750 miles we had driven three months earlier to the Kansas church cemetery.

In that time of intense pain, Marshall and I clung to each other. Every day I needed to talk about Mandy—to recall the smoothness of her skin, the scent of Baby Magic shampoo in her hair, the physical ordeals she suffered with cataracts, glaucoma, surgeries, feeding tubes, and other painful medical procedures.

I felt as if I had lost not only my daughter but my identity as well. For two years, my job and my *calling* had been to care for her. My closest friends were those who had helped care for her—at church, at the doctors' offices, at Easter Seals. My support group had centered on Mandy—and now that center was gone. I missed those friends.

For two years, every hour had been filled by taking care of her needs. Now Stacey and Kelsey were in school, Marshall went back to work, and my hours and my house were empty. Suddenly I went from having no time to having too much time.

Our church family offered thoughtful support, including meals and cards and phone calls assuring us of their prayers. I drew some comfort from the Bible's promise of heaven and knowing that one day I would see my children again. But in the weeks right after Mandy's death, that comfort felt hollow. Why couldn't I be with Mandy and Toby *now?* Were they OK?

I read every Bible reference to heaven. I devoured Christian books on what awaits us in eternity. But still the nagging question lingered: If God couldn't take better care of them on earth, how could I be sure they were OK in heaven?

As a mother, I needed to know, beyond a doubt, that my children were safe and loved. I needed something more than a pat on the arm and a "Don't worry, God will provide." I needed God to touch not just my head but my soul.

I visited Mary Lou Bayly, a wise Christian woman who had seen her husband and three of her children die. I needed to talk with someone who had experienced multiple losses. I told her about my doubts.

"I didn't struggle with that same issue," she said. "I had other questions. But one thing I have learned: As the Bible says, 'You have not because you ask not.' Whatever you truly need, ask the Lord for it. But be prepared for God to answer in unexpected ways."

For the next three nights, I lay awake praying that God would give me some assurance that Toby and Mandy were OK. The third night, I was praying that prayer when I heard footsteps coming down the hall. This wasn't unusual—our daughters Stacey, seven, and Kelsey, four, often wanted to crawl into bed with Mom and Dad. But this time the footsteps came to the door of our room, stopped, then went back down the hall to the girls' room.

The next morning, Palm Sunday, I tried to awaken Stacey, but she complained she was too sleepy to get up.

"You wouldn't happen to know anything about a midnight wanderer who came to our room last night, would you?" I asked.

Suddenly Stacey was wide awake. "Oh, yes. That was me. I came to your room to tell you that God spoke to me, but you were asleep, so I went back to bed."

"I wasn't asleep, honey. You could have come in.... Wait a minute. God spoke to you? What did he say?" I was dubious.

"He said that Mandy and Toby are very busy, that they are preparing our house, and they are guarding his throne."

"How did God say these things?"

"He spoke to my mind," Stacey replied matter-of-factly. "Then when I thought you were asleep, I came back to my bed and repeated the words over and over so I could remember to tell you. It seemed like an important message."

I didn't know what to make of it. Stacey has never, before or since, gotten such a message from God.

As I reflected on it, though, I realized my prayer for assurance had been answered. I don't know what I'd been expecting. A dream? A vision? Some new insight that would miraculously take all my cares away? But by speaking through a seven-year-old, God had done the unexpected. My worries about Mandy and Toby were gone!

They weren't just OK, they were *busy*. They were preparing

for us. And they were together, close to Jesus.

This is all consistent with Scripture. We know heaven is not just a place of being but a place of doing, of activity for God's glory. We know places in heaven are being prepared for us. We know Jesus enjoyed having children near him. We know "the least shall be greatest," and I can't think of many people more "least" than Toby and Mandy.

No, the grief didn't vanish. I still long to see my precious little ones. Tears still well up at unexpected times. But I also know that God provided the assurance I needed that he is taking care of them. I now live with one foot in heaven and one foot on earth, and it's not a bad way to live.

Even after that amazing answer to prayer, we had more "grief work" to do. Our whole family went to a six-week support group for those who have lost a family member. That helped us deal with our losses and gave us ways to communicate in words and symbols. (We still make sure Mandy's stuffed Winnie-the-Pooh and Toby's "little bear" are in all our family photos.)

In addition, I became part of Compassionate Friends, an ongoing support group for women who have lost children. I needed to talk through feelings, questions, and struggles with other mothers who could assure me I wasn't the only one who felt this way. For almost a year, this group met that significant need.

But by far the biggest issue Marshall and I faced was whether we should try to have another child. Relatives on both sides of the family were adamantly against the idea. Even though Mandy's microcephaly and Toby's Trisomy 13 were completely unrelated, so far as any medical or genetic experts could tell us, some of our loved ones told us we would be foolish and irresponsible to risk another pregnancy.

But Marshall and I had an unmistakable sense that the story wasn't over yet. Even if our next child were to have Trisomy 13 or microcephaly, we were ready. Mandy and Toby had been deeply loved. We'd be honored to accept another such child.

Just over a year after we said farewell to Mandy, we said hello to an active and healthy boy we named Bayly. He has brought joy, healing, and the usual chaos into our lives.

Mandy and Toby are still members of our family—they just aren't living with us right now. We remember them daily and talk about them frequently. I'm grateful for every moment I was with them, and I long to see them again. And while our marriage and our faith were shaken, they have both emerged more unshakable than before.

Commentary

Handicapped kids are a unique challenge to a marriage relationship. They also provide a unique opportunity for trust to develop and love to grow. At the outset Susan and Marshall determined that they weren't going to be one of the divorce statistics, but they experienced enough of the tensions to recognize the danger. Imagine the stress and strain, both individually and as a family, from learning how to deal with, in Susan's words, "a life-and-death condition that doesn't end."

We all know that men and women are different. However, a crisis situation can magnify those differences and lead to increased misunderstanding, miscommunication, and conflict. Some of the many things that Susan and Marshall did right were to acknowledge those differences, identify the conflicts, redefine roles, and work through them. They worked on trying to see the world through each other's eyes. They also maintained a sense of humor. God can use humor to provide strength and perspective.

Over the years, I've had the privilege of walking through similar valleys with many couples. Most of those couples didn't merely survive the experience. Like Susan and Marshall they *got* through it because they *grew* through it. The story of Susan and Marshall illustrates several keys to keeping your head above water during a flood of pain. They made a decision, sometimes several times a day, to keep committed to the relationship. They dealt with the grief issues in the family and acknowledged and allowed for each other's differences. Susan sought wisdom from a wise Christian woman, and they in turn used their experience to be a help to others. Their family went to a six-week support group for those who have lost a family member and Susan became a part of Compassionate Friends. Finally, after much prayer and soul-searching, they trusted God and became open to trying for another child.

As I read Susan and Marshall's story I was struck with not only their endurance but also with their perseverance. In *My Utmost for His Highest*, Oswald Chambers writes that perseverance is more than endurance. It starts with endurance but it is combined with an absolute assurance and trust that what we are looking for is going to happen.

Sometimes, people in crisis can write a letter to family and friends to help them understand the situation. Here is an abridgement of a sample letter I've shared with a number of couples; alter it to fit your situation:

Dear Friend (family, pastor, fellow workers ...),

Recently I have suffered a devastating loss. I am grieving and it will take months and even years to recover from this loss. I wanted to let you know some of what I expect during this time of recovery.

I will cry from time to time. My tears are a sign that I am recovering. At times you may see me angry for no apparent reason. My emotions are intense because of my grief. If I don't always make sense to you, please be forgiving and patient with me. And if I repeat myself again and again, please accept this as normal.

More than anything I need your understanding and your presence. You don't always have to know what to say or even say anything if you don't know how to respond. Your presence and a touch or hug helps me. Please don't wait for me to call you since sometimes I am too tired or too tearful to do so.

If I tend to withdraw from you, please don't let me do that. I need you to reach out to me for several months.

Pray for me that I would come to see meaning in my loss someday and that I would know God's comfort and love. It does help to let me know that you are praying for me.

If you have experienced a similar type of loss, please feel free to share it with me. It will help rather than cause me to feel worse. And don't stop sharing if I begin to cry. It's all right and any tears you express as we talk are all right, too.

Thank you for caring about me. Thank you for listening and praying. Your concern comforts me and is a gift for which I will always be thankful.

(modified from Deits, *Life After Loss*, 150-51, used by permission of the author as given in his book)

What can you do for someone who is bereaved and dealing with a loss? Norm Wright, in his invaluable book *Crisis Counseling*, advises:

1. Begin where the bereaved person is and not where you think he or she should be.
2. Clarify their expressed feelings with them by restating their words and their emotions in your own words.
3. Empathize with them, feel with them, be present with their pain and loss.
4. Be sensitive to their feelings, and don't say too much.
5. Don't use faulty reassurances such as "You'll feel better in a few days" or "It won't hurt so much after awhile."

If you or a family you know is facing a similar crisis, share this story with them. Call them and pray with them on the phone. Encourage them to make sure there is a time each day, perhaps even a small time, when they pray together. Ask often if there is any way you can help. Maybe you could arrange for helpers to come into their home on a weekly basis so that they can have some time away for dates, errands, and exercise. Yes, exercise! It helps during times of stress and strain.

If you are in a similar situation, my prayer is that you will experience what Susan and Marshall experienced. In Susan's words: "While our marriage and our faith were shaken, they have both emerged more unshakable than before." That's a great example of what Paul meant when he told us that our God can cause all things to work together for good.

Resources

Lloyd Ahlem, *How to Cope* (Glendale, Calif.: Regal, 1978).

Bob Deits, *Life After Loss: A Personal Guide Dealing with Death, Divorce, Job Change, and Relocation* (Tucson, Ariz.: Fisher, 1992).

H. Norman Wright, *Crisis Counseling: Helping People in Crisis and Stress* (San Bernardino, Calif.: Here's Life Publishers, 1985).

H. Norman Wright & Joyce Wright, *I'll Love You Forever* (Colorado Springs, Colo.: Focus on the Family, 1993).

Chapter 13

Natural Disaster
by Gregg Lewis

W hen Hurricane Hugo body-slammed the U.S. Virgin Islands, I followed CNN's twenty-four-hour news coverage with intense personal interest. My brother Mark, his wife, Angela, and their two little girls lived on St. Croix.

A ham radio operator from Atlanta finally called my parents after five days with the cryptic report—Mark, Angela, and children OK. House destroyed.

This is their story.

Angela: A friend told me, "This may be a hundred-year hurricane." Having lived in the islands for just over a year, and never having experienced a hurricane, I had no concept of what that meant.

Mark: After work on Friday I collected toys, lawn furniture, and other loose items from the yard and stashed them under the deck. I also boarded up the windows on the north and east sides of the house. By Saturday morning, the radio reports were warning people to have everything ready before nightfall. We spent the entire day in preparation, boarding up the rest of the windows and doing various other things. The work wasn't difficult, and we did it with an air of anticipation and excitement.

Angela: Some of our friends planned to go to community shelters just before the storm arrived. We weren't sure what we should do until sometime on Saturday when I heard an "expert" on the radio advising people in homes with concrete walls and in elevations above the expected tidal surge to stay where they were rather than crowd the public shelters unnecessarily. That report, which I relayed to Mark, pretty much decided things for us. Most of our walls were concrete and our house sat on a mountain ridge, a mile or so inland from St. Croix's north shore.

Mark: When Sunday dawned, the storm was still hours away. But the wind had picked up to thirty-plus miles per hour. I'd seen pictures of a Jamaican hurricane where people had to dodge flying coconuts. So I took my machete, lopped all the fruit off the palm tree in front of our house, and stored the coconuts on our back porch. By late afternoon, fifty- to sixty-mile-per-hour gusts were bending some of the smaller trees to the ground. From the deck on the front of our house I watched huge waves crashing onto the north shore of St. Croix. It was time to go inside and wait.

Angela: Since the girls' bedroom was a wooden addition on the back of the house, we moved six-month-old Ivey's crib into our room and put three-year-old Frederica down for the night in our bed. Mark stayed with the girls while I went into the dining room and sat down to look through a newspaper by candlelight.

A couple of times I thought I felt a fine mist on my face. Looking around I decided it must be my imagination. I later rejoined the rest of the family in the bedroom and Mark went to check on how things were going.

Mark: I'd gone into the dining room and was heading for the study when I thought I saw some movement above me. I did a double take. Nothing. Then it happened again. The roof lifted, just an inch or so, and then settled back. At least that's what it looked like. A little while later it happened again. I ran to the bedroom to tell Angela I needed her help. "The roof's starting to go!"

Angela: Mark has a very calm personality. So hearing the alarm and the intensity in his voice shook me. I took Ivey in one arm, picked up a flashlight, and followed my husband out of the bedroom.

"Up there! See it?" he exclaimed.

I didn't want to, but I did. As the wind gusted, the entire roof section gently surged upward. I could see the sky through a two-inch crack and felt a fine mist of rain blow into the room.

Mark: I ran through the study into the back storage room to grab my nail belt, some boards, and a stepladder. Then I raced back into the dining room. I decided to try to tie the roof into some wooden door frames. Angela balanced a squirming, crying baby on one hip while shining a flashlight for me to see.

It's hard enough hammering nails in the dark, but with the roof surging up and down, it seemed almost impossible. And even after I got the corners anchored, the middle of the roof still rose and fell with each gust.

Having done all I could in the dining room, I headed back through the study again, only to see that section of roof lifting just like the other one. I got more boards and tied the rafters in the study to the door frames in that room. But by the time I finished, I realized everything I had done was temporary at best. We were still early in the storm; the roof wouldn't hold.

Angela: We figured the bathroom, a small inner room with concrete walls all around, would be the safest place in the house. So Mark took the mattress out of the baby bed and put it on the bathroom floor. Then he picked a sleeping Frederica out of our bed and lay down beside her on the crib mattress. I reclined on a few pillows we tossed onto the bathroom floor and tried to nurse my crying infant back to sleep.

We decided that, if the roof began to go, we would each take a child and get into the concrete shower compartment to sit on the Coleman cooler where we'd stashed water, crackers and a few other supplies. I nodded agreement. It was about ten o'clock.

Mark: We hadn't been in the bathroom more than fifteen minutes when we heard a ripping noise. By the time I snatched up Frederica, Angela had bounded past me with Ivey into the shower stall. As I stepped in after her with Frederica, I reached back and grabbed the crib mattress I'd been lying on and pulled it over the opening of the shower stall.

I thought I heard the popping sound of the braces I'd nailed into the rafters. Then came the deafening sound of ripping and splintering wood as section after section of the roof tore away. Boards, ceiling, even chunks of concrete crashed down where we'd been lying only seconds before. Within a minute or so, two feet of debris covered the floor outside the shower.

Immediately following the terrifying sound of the roof ripping off came a startlingly loud shatter. Angela jumped. "What was that?"

"Probably the mirror in the dining room," I said. But a bigger crash followed as the wind tore the deck off the front of the house and with it the boarded-up frame of the sliding glass doors in the dining room. Crash followed crash as all the windows on the ocean side of the house shattered from the inside. And even as the sounds of destruction continued around us, the storm raged louder and stronger outside that three-by-three-foot shower stall.

Angela: I don't know if it was the awful crashing of the windows, the terrifying roar of the storm, or the baby's screaming that awakened Frederica. But she began to whimper, "Where are we?" When Mark explained we were in the shower, she wanted to know why.

"Because," Mark assured her calmly, "the hurricane is here and this is the safest place in the house." With one hand holding the crib mattress over our heads and the other arm snuggling Frederica, Mark leaned close to her and began to sing. Amazingly, she dropped back to sleep.

Sitting jammed tight next to Mark on the cooler, I had a

harder time quieting Ivey. Finding a comfortable position to nurse her proved impossible. But I finally shifted around long enough to begin nursing and she too settled down.

Mark: Sitting there, cramped and helpless, time seemed to creep minute by minute. With each five minutes, ten minutes, especially each thirty minutes we knew, at least we hoped, the storm was passing by and we felt grateful. Yet I wondered how the wind could keep blowing that way for so long. Midnight. One o'clock. Two o'clock. And it seemed that the hurricane continued to grow stronger. We found out later that the sustained winds eventually reached 165 miles per hour. The reason it went on so long was that the storm's forward progress slowed to between one and two miles per hour, meaning Hugo stood almost still for hours while it hammered St. Croix.

As a builder I knew that the integrity of any house's structure depends on the integrity of its central bond beam. The friend who had rented us this house had told us she'd once had a fire. And in making my own plans to do some remodeling for her, I'd found a number of weaknesses in the basic structure. With the roof gone, I wasn't at all sure how much the walls could take.

When I had envisioned the possibility of the roof blowing off I'd known what we should do: Get into the bathroom. But when I considered the possibility of those walls going, I kept searching my mind for some safer place. I could think of no recourse at all, and still the fierceness of the storm grew. Until, a little after three o'clock, it suddenly stopped.

Angela: We wondered if it could finally be over. Or, a terrible thought: "Was this just the storm's eye?" We used the opportunity to stand up and stretch our aching muscles for the first time in more than five hours. We stepped out into the debris-strewn bathroom for a moment. But we didn't dare go far for fear the storm might resume just as quickly as it had stopped.

Within minutes it exploded again at full force. When the wind hit us from the south for the first time, it brought with it the sound of hail. At least we thought it was hail until we realized that the slivers and teardrops dripping down the shower walls weren't ice, but bits of glass churned up by the changing wind.

Mark: On the positive side, we now had a pretty good idea how long the storm would last. Figuring we'd had five hours of the worst wind before the eye, we stood to have another five hours before it was over. On the negative side, the winds now blasted at our weakened structure from the opposite direction as hard or harder than they had before.

I could feel the shower wall trembling under the constant onslaught of the steady winds. The periodic 200-mile-per-hour gusts scared me. There was no way to anticipate when the next one would hit. And each gust felt like a sledgehammer pounding against the outside of the shower stall.

I've been through some scary moments in my life—automobile accidents, for example—where I experienced intense fear for short bursts of time. But I've never felt anything like those hours of relentless terror in the face of this incredible force. Angela and I sat for hour after hour on a fine line between life and death with our two children on our laps.

Angela: Strange as it seems, I don't think I ever considered the possibility that we might be killed. The strong emotion I was feeling seemed parallel to my feelings during childbirth. This too was a tiny drama that confined me in time and place where I was completely at the mercy of an unpredictable and uncontrollable force. The best I could hope to do was monitor my own reactions and concentrate on maintaining control of my feelings.

While I was glad to have Mark there with me, it wasn't as if I could depend on him to intervene to protect me from what was happening. So although we were crammed tightly together in that shower stall, the experience in some ways felt intensely private—just the storm and me and God.

Mark had surprised me before the calm of the storm's eye by asking, "Have you been praying?" When I told him I had, he assured me he was, too.

After the second half of the storm began, Mark was praying out loud. Over and over I heard him say, "Give us peace. Give us courage. Wrap your arms around this house."

Mark: I didn't get too elaborate with my thoughts or my prayers. I kept trying to think of something else I could do or somewhere else we could go. I prayed repeatedly for wisdom to know what to do and the courage to do it. I envisioned God's hands around the house, protecting us and holding up the walls. And finally, I prayed that Angela and the girls would be spared. I was so uncertain I'd make it I told Angela that if she was trapped in the bathroom after the storm, she could easily kick the slats out of the louvered door and crawl out.

As Monday dawned, the walls still shook. The worst of the

gusts seemed to be slacking off but the winds remained too dangerous to venture out. So we stayed put.

Not until after nine o'clock did I finally risk a one-man reconnaissance trip out into the storm's gradually slackening winds. The relief that came with the realization that we had survived was quickly tempered by what I saw.

The entire living room had blown away. The majority of our remaining earthly possessions looked like they'd been blenderized with equal parts glass, wood, assorted building materials, and rainwater to create an ugly, soupy, and smelly hurricane stew.

Stepping outside proved even more depressing. What had been a lush tropical paradise now looked like nuclear winter. Everywhere I looked down the mountain, trails of debris spread out from where houses used to be. Could we be the only people alive on the entire island?

Using my machete, I whacked a trail through the brush to reach our nearest neighbor. He had survived with several dry rooms, and he offered us temporary refuge. So I headed back home to get Angela and the girls.

Angela: Before I'd even set foot out of the shower stall, Mark warned me, "It's like the holocaust out here." And it was. But as I climbed over kitchen cabinets and waded through what seemed like all our earthly possessions, I kept telling myself none of those things mattered. What did matter was that our family was alive and safe and together. For more than eleven hours we'd huddled in a shower stall with nothing but a crib mattress between us and one of the worst hurricanes in history.

And we had survived! That was more than enough reason to be grateful.

That shared sentiment and very little else sustained Mark and Angela the next few days as they salvaged what they could from the remains of their possessions. With almost no usable food, none to be found on St. Croix and no relief supplies arriving for days, they bartered the use of their portable generator for meals with neighbors and friends.

On the sixth day after Hugo, Angela and the children flew back to the States to stay with relatives while Mark stayed on to do what he could to rebuild the island. Telling his boss he saw more important work to be done than putting roofs on the vacation homes of millionaires, he quit his job as a construction supervisor and volunteered his services to the Virgin Islands Assistant Commissioner of Health. One week after the hurricane, he was put in charge of the distribution of emergency medical supplies for the island.

Six weeks after Hugo, Angela and the girls returned and moved into a small house Mark had found. For three months they lived without electricity. Five months passed before phone service was restored to their part of the island. And both Mark and Angela say the lessons learned from the hurricane will far outlast the inconveniences of the physical recovery.

Mark: For me, our Hugo experience left a change of perspective on time and values. Our family emerging from that shower stall alive was really the most important thing. Anything we could pick out of the debris, any clothes we could find to wash—that was all just a bonus.

The need for a car without dents now seems absurd. All those things that are part of our middle-class American lifestyle, all those details that demand so much of our time and energy, don't matter. They're not reality at all. Not compared to life and relationships, marriage or family.

When it comes to marriage, an experience like ours, which has been like a graduate course in crisis management, puts the mundane, day-to-day struggles into perspective. It made us more tolerant of petty differences and irritations. It gave us an appreciation of each other that helps keep us out of the doldrums of a relationship.

Angela: I still appreciate nice things. But they no longer truly matter because of the perspective we gained in that shower stall during what has come to be called here in the islands "the longest night."

During those dark, horrible hours, Hugo stripped us bare and forced us to face the emotional and spiritual reality of life. It changed us in more ways than I can explain. But I see an added dimension of strength in Mark as a husband and a father that I never saw before; I love him more than ever.

In fact, just a day or two after the hurricane, while we were without food, clothing, or a home, Mark looked at me very tenderly and said, "You know, to get to this point in marriage a lot of couples just go to a marriage enrichment weekend; we go through a life-and-death experience." And we laughed.

But it's true. Six months after Hugo, it's like I had a new husband. And we have a new marriage.

And for all of this, as well as for our family's survival, we have to give all the thanks to God.

Commentary

Throughout this book we've met couples who have experienced the hurricane force of financial, moral, spiritual, and relational crises. Sometimes the emotional force of these kinds of crises can be greater than the physical wind of a hurricane. However, in the story of Mark and Angela the opportunity for building trust was an actual hurricane. I've never been through a hurricane, but after reading their story I've decided that's as close as I want to get.

Psychiatrist Joy Joffe defines a survivor as someone who, after having been knocked down, "knows how to stay down until the count of nine and then to get up differently. The nonsurvivor gets up right away and gets hit again."

The experience of Mark and Angela is a classic illustration of the fact that the best time to deal with a crisis is *before* you find yourself in the middle of one. That's right! You don't need to wait until the roof is blowing down and the walls are crumbling around you to deal with it. In Matthew 6:25-34 Christ gives us three simple habits we can cultivate that are guaranteed to be helpful during a crisis.

The first habit is to cultivate a divine perspective, make sure your spiritual values are in control. Bathe your mind in some of God's many promises. Write verses such as Psalm 37:1-9, Matthew 6:33, Romans 8:28-29a, 1 Corinthians 10:13, Philippians 4:4-9, 13, 19, on three-by-five cards and carry them in your purse or coat pocket.

The second habit is to ask God to help you learn how to accept what can't be changed. There are three categories of circumstances. The first is things we can control or change. The second is things we cannot change but can influence. The third is things that we cannot change or influence—things that we can do absolutely nothing about.

The third way to prepare for a crisis is to learn how to live one day at a time. This key principle is articulated by our Lord in his Sermon on the Mount: "So don't worry about tomorrow, for tomorrow will bring its own worries. Today's trouble is enough for today" (Mt 6:34, NLT). I find it significant that "One day at a time" has become the motto of Alcoholics Anonymous, the world's most effective recovery group.

Going through crisis, in and of itself, does not necessarily guarantee good communication, deeper love, and increased intimacy. It is not in and of itself a trust builder. It's *how* we go through it. As we allow God to go before us, come alongside us, and be with us through the dark and difficult times, our love and trust can grow.

One day a friend of mine watched a father playing with his little boy. He repeatedly threw him in the air and caught him just before he hit the ground. The child was relaxed and having a great time saying, "Do it again! Do it again!"

My friend thought, "If that were me, I'd be stiff as a board." He then turned and asked the father, "Can you explain why he's so relaxed, even when he's out of control?" The father paused and then responded, "It's very simple. We have a history together. We've played this game before, and I've never dropped him."

The hurricane blew away Angela and Mark's temporal foundation and their temporal security. But how they chose to respond allowed them to strengthen their real foundation and increase their trust. Through their faith, commitment, and hard work they turned what could have been a trust breaker into a trust builder. So can you.

Resources

Lloyd Ahlem, *How to Cope* (Glendale, Calif.: Regal, 1978).
Don Hawkins, *Never Give Up* (Lincoln, Neb.: Back to the Bible, 1995).
H. Norman Wright, *How to Have a Creative Crisis* (Waco, Tex.: Word, 1986).

Conclusion

The national seal of Australia features two unusual animals: the emu and the kangaroo. Neither has the ability to move backward. They can only go forward. The large tail of the kangaroo keeps it from backing up. The emu is an ostrichlike bird and its feet have only three toes. If it tries to back up it falls over. What do an emu and a kangaroo have to do with building trust?

When discouragement or depression or death or despair knock on your door, you have the opportunity to decide if you are going to try to go backward, stay stuck, or move ahead. You have the opportunity to decide what you are going to allow the situation to do *to* you or do *for* you. You have the opportunity to decide whether you are going to be a victim or a victor. You have the opportunity to decide whether you want to be conquered or, with God's help, to become more than a conqueror. If you want to learn, if you want to grow, if you want to experience victory, you must make a decision to reach out, take God's hand, and take the next step forward.

It all starts with making a decision. Faith is nothing more than a matter of making decisions. Billy Graham has stated, "Decision is the most important word in the English language." For this reason, he named his radio program "The Hour of

Decision," and he named his magazine *Decision*.

The couples in this book have faced an overwhelming array of problems. Some of them were caused by their own sin and selfishness, some were cause by immaturity and weakness, and some came about because we are all fallen people living in a fallen world. Regardless of the cause, each person and each couple was faced with many decisions. It is what they decided to do that made a difference in their relationships.

These couples also learned that it doesn't matter how old you are, how smart you are, how spiritual you are, how many degrees you have, how much money you make, or how much success you've enjoyed. No one is excused from the school of hard knocks.

The couples that you've met in these pages are part of a growing chorus of men and women who will tell you that strong, healthy, and intimate marriages do not know deep levels of trust *in spite of* problems but *because of* what they have allowed God to teach them as they've gone through these trials.